Museums, Infinity and the Culture of Protocols

Museums, Infinity and the Culture of Protocols enters a dialogue about museums' responsibility for the curation of their collections into an infinite future while also tackling contentious issues of repatriation and digital access to collections.

Bringing into focus a number of key debates centred on ethnographic collections and their relationship with source communities, Morphy considers the value material objects have to different 'local' communities – the museum and the source community – and the value-creation processes with which they are entangled. The focus on values and value brings the issue of repatriation and access into a dialogue between the two locals, questioning who has access to collections and whose values are taken into consideration. Placing the museum itself firmly at the centre of the debate, Morphy posits that museums constitute a kind of 'local' embedded in a trajectory of value.

Museums, Infinity and the Culture of Protocols challenges aspects of postcolonial theory that position museums in the past by presenting an argument that places relationships with communities as central to the future of museums. This makes the book essential reading for academics and students working in the fields of museum and heritage studies, anthropology, archaeology, Indigenous studies, cultural studies, and history.

Howard Morphy is an Emeritus Professor and Head of the Centre for Digital Humanities Research at the Australian National University. In his career he has moved between museums and university departments and feels at home in collections and archives as much as in the field. He spent ten years at the Pitt Rivers Museum, Oxford University, as curator and lecturer. In 2013 he was awarded the Huxley Medal of the Royal Anthropological Institute.

Museums in Focus

Series Editor: Kylie Message

The Australian National University, Australia

Committed to the articulation of big, even risky, ideas in small format publications, 'Museums in Focus' challenges authors and readers to experiment with, innovate, and press museums and the intellectual frameworks through which we view these. It offers a platform for approaches that radically rethink the relationships between cultural and intellectual dissent and crisis and debates about museums, politics and the broader public sphere.

'Museums in Focus' is motivated by the intellectual hypothesis that museums are not innately 'useful', safe' or even 'public' places, and that recalibrating our thinking about them might benefit from adopting a more radical and oppositional form of logic and approach. Examining this problem requires a level of comfort with (or at least tolerance of) the idea of crisis, dissent, protest and radical thinking, and authors might benefit from considering how cultural and intellectual crisis, regeneration and anxiety have been dealt with in other disciplines and contexts.

Museums, Infinity and the Culture of Protocols
Ethnographic Collections and Source Communities
Howard Morphy

Anti-Museum
Adrian Franklin

Queering the Museum
Nikki Sullivian and Craig Middleton

www.routledge.com/Museums-in-Focus/book-series/MIF

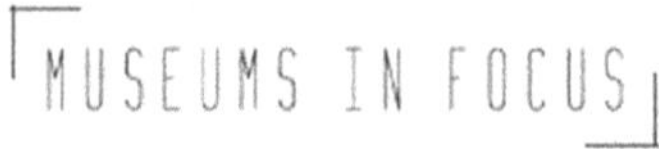

Logo by James Verdon (2017)

Museums, Infinity and the Culture of Protocols

Ethnographic Collections and Source Communities

Howard Morphy

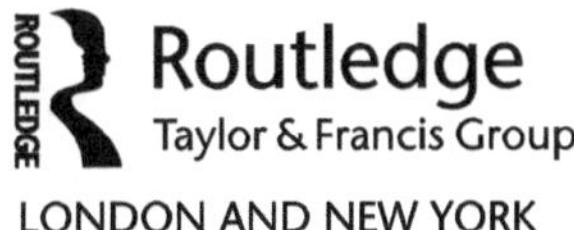

LONDON AND NEW YORK

First published 2020
by Routledge
2 Park Square, Milton Park, Abingdon, Oxon OX14 4RN

and by Routledge
605 Third Avenue, New York, NY 10017

First issued in paperback 2021

Routledge is an imprint of the Taylor & Francis Group, an informa business

British Library Cataloguing-in-Publication Data
A catalogue record for this book is available from the British Library

Library of Congress Cataloging-in-Publication Data
A catalog record for this book has been requested

ISBN 13: 978-1-03-208713-9 (pbk)
ISBN 13: 978-1-138-56559-3 (hbk)

Typeset in Times New Roman
by Apex CoVantage, LLC

Contents

Figures

Acknowledgements

This book builds on ideas that I have developed over many years. The chapters are either new or substantially rewritten. Chapter 5 is a revised version of my chapter 'Open Access Versus the Culture of Protocols' in Raymond A Silverman's book *Museum as Process*, published in 2015 by Routledge, and much of the argument for Chapter 4 was developed in 'Scientific Knowledge and Rights in Skeletal Remains – Dilemmas in the Curation of "Other" People's Bones' in Paul Turnbull and Michael Pickering's edited book *The Long Way Home: The Meaning and Values of Repatriation*, published in 2010 by Berghahn. Many people contributed in different ways to add substance to my arguments, including Lindy Allen, Philip Batty, Josh Bell, Jeremy Coote, Jason Gibson, Joseph Gumbula, Louise Hamby, Jessica De Largy Healy, Gwyneira Isaac, Kylie Message, Daphne Nash, Laura Peers, Michael Pickering, Ray Silverman, Paul Turnbull, Karen Westmacott, and Andrea Witcomb. I owe a particular debt to Bree Blakeman, Anna Edmundson, Frances Morphy, and Gaye Sculthorpe, who read the manuscript as a whole and gave me invaluable feedback that in some cases saved me from egregious errors. The research upon which much of this book is based was funded by grants from the Australian Research Council. Writing and researching the book was greatly facilitated by residence as a visiting scholar at the Center for Advanced Study in the Behavioural Sciences, Stanford, and as scholar at the Getty Research Center in Los Angeles.

1 Introduction

Living with museums

This book comes out of a lifelong engagement with museums. As a child, I was lucky enough to visit the Pitt Rivers Museum in Oxford where I regularly found myself transported into other people's lives and into the richness and diversity of their worlds. I marvelled at the Yoruba carved portrait of Queen Victoria, wished that the costumes could be mine to dress up in. I entered the doors of model Burmese village houses and stood transfixed before the shrunken heads. I was intrigued by the label which reads,

> Silvered and stoppered glass flask. Said to contain a witch. Obtained about 1915 from an old lady living in a village near HOVE, SUSSEX.

The label went on to warn me that 'they do say there be a witch in it, and if you let un out there'll be a peck o'trouble'.

Like James Fenton (1982), I too found nervous memories evoked by the placard: TAKE NOTICE MEN-TRAPS AND SPRING-GUNS ARE SET ON THESE PREMISES.

In my case, it was the fear of formidable iron jaws awaiting my leg on childhood trespass through copses on the edge of the nearby Blenheim estates.

The typological displays at the Pitt Rivers Museum flattened the differences between time and place. As a child, I did not see the imprint of colonization and did not walk away with an evolutionary message of progress but rather with a sense of delight at the magic of the place touched by a sense of danger. In Fenton's words my experience of the museum was that

> We cannot either feel that we have come
>   Far or in any particular direction.

***

My entanglement with museums continued. I studied anthropology at University College London, and in 1979 undertook an M. Phil. thesis supervised by Peter Ucko. The subject of my thesis was the analysis, at a distance, of the *toas* of the Australian Aboriginal people of the Lake Eyre region of central Australia, which were in the collections of the South Australian Museum. *Toas* are exquisite objects whose main function was said to be as direction signs. They had been collected at the turn of the nineteenth and twentieth centuries by a Lutheran missionary, R. G. Reuther, from Killalpannina near Lake Eyre. Reuther's manuscripts reveal an Aboriginal population in crisis, victims of the continual and, on occasion, murderous encroachment on their country by pastoralists moving onto the desert region from the south following a deceptive period of good rainfall.

Bob Edwards, at the time the curator of the South Australian Museum, facilitated my research. I obtained a grant which covered the cost of photographing the nearly 500 objects, and the museum sent me copies of the manuscripts I needed. My approach to *toas* was semiological (Morphy 1977). I analyzed them as a system of communication to understand how they 'spoke'. I became aware of the incredible resource provided by well-documented collections and took my first steps to becoming involved in the dialogue between art and artefact. The *toas*, which in the 1960s had been largely unrecognized as aesthetic forms, emerged in the 1980s as art objects in a major exhibition, *Art and Land*, at the South Australian Museum (Jones and Sutton 1986).

***

My first job was as a research assistant in the then Ethnography Department of the British Museum; at the time, it began its brief existence as the Museum of Mankind. One of the opening exhibitions was *The Australian Aborigine* curated by Bryan Cranstone. His great interest was in the history of technology, and the focus of the exhibition was very much on the material culture of a hunting and gathering society. I felt the absence of the richness of the artistic, social, and religious life that I had come to know from my research on *toas* and from Phylis Kaberry's lectures at University College London on the complexity of Australian Aboriginal kinship. But I respected Cranstone's concern that an emphasis on art might impose a limited and European view on Aboriginal material culture. His long-time colleague and keeper of the department, William Fagg, had no such qualms. He had been at the forefront of the recognition of African art, and many of the exhibitions at the museum celebrated its aesthetic qualities in addition to emphasizing their cultural context.

***

Although I appreciated greatly the opportunity to work in the British Museum's collections, I also wanted to understand art and material culture in the context of production. The *toas* had allowed me to enter what was to me then a distant time and place. I wanted to work with people as they were making art in the present. I was fortunate enough to get a scholarship at the Australian National University (ANU) to undertake a fieldwork-based doctorate on Australian Aboriginal art. The prehistorian John Mulvaney, head of the newly established Department of Prehistory and Anthropology, wanted me to study bark paintings as artefacts produced for sale in the context of change. In preparation for fieldwork, I photographed the major collections of bark paintings in Australian museum collections and undertook a formal analysis of them. I sensed in the bark paintings of the Yolngu people of eastern Arnhem Land the same deep semiotic and spiritual mapping of land that the *toas* conveyed.

In 1973, I had the opportunity to visit Yirrkala for a week, accompanying the Reverend Edgar Wells, who had received a grant to document some of the very same paintings I had photographed in museum collections. The Reverend Wilbur Chaseling had been the founding missionary at Yirrkala in 1935, and the sale of bark paintings to museums was one of the ways in which the mission covered its costs. It was his collection in museums in Sydney, Melbourne, and Brisbane that Wells wished to document.

Wells had been the superintendent at Yirrkala 30 years after Chaseling. He was a passionate advocate for Yolngu art and became involved in marketing it to the world outside. But he also saw it as a testament to Yolngu spirituality. He was a builder of churches, and in the new church he built at Yirrkala in 1962, at the suggestion of Yolngu, he commissioned clan leaders to paint two panels of their *miny'tji* (paintings) to be installed on either side of the altar. Wells soon found himself working closely with Yolngu in resisting the threat to their land posed by the discovery of large bauxite reserves. In 1963, the Church Panels became the inspiration for the Bark Petition sent to Parliament demanding, among other things, that Yolngu ownership of their land should be recognized. Although land rights legislation was still over a decade away, the Bark Petition played a major role in the political process that led to its eventual existence.

I had an incredibly privileged introduction to Yolngu society. Edgar Wells was seen as a strong advocate of the struggle for land rights and deeply appreciative of Yolngu art. On that first visit, we spent an evening together with Wandjuk Marika, soon to become chairman of the Aboriginal Arts Board, and Narritjin Maymuru, who painted the Bark Petition that is today in Parliament House in Canberra.

Six months later, I returned to Yirrkala. One evening, early on, sitting with Narrijtin, I began to thumb through a set of Yolngu paintings from museum collections, turning each over in turn. A number of the paintings had been collected by the anthropologist Donald Thomson between 1937 and 1943. After a while, Narritjin looked at me and said, 'I know what you are trying to do. You are trying to show that our art has changed. We will show you that it has not'. It took me many years and several books to fully appreciate what Narritjin meant. But what I realized at once was that despite the rupture of the colonial encounter, Yolngu people felt no sense of discontinuity between their past and their present. The bark paintings in the museum collections were, in the Yolngu view, part of a continuing present.

***

I completed my doctorate in 1978, and for the next nine years taught at the ANU. My connection with museums and exhibitions continued. Narritjin Maymuru and his son Banapana came to the ANU as H. C. Coombs Creative Arts Fellows. After the Aboriginal Land Rights Act (Northern Territory) 1976 was passed, Frances Morphy and I were seconded from the ANU to work on the Yuṯpundji Djindiwirritj (Roper Bar) Land claim. With Stephen Wilde, I organized a conference called Aboriginal Art in Contemporary Australia. To coincide with the conference, we held an exhibition of works for sale, working in collaboration with the Aboriginal art centres that were being established across Australia. Many of the works were acquired by the National Gallery of Australia. And then I returned to England and Oxford in 1986, where I had been offered a position as a curator at the Pitt Rivers Museum.

Back at Pitt Rivers, I resisted the temptation to remove the stopper from the witch's bottle. But I had arrived at an exciting time. I had agreed, before leaving Australia, to give a paper at the International Union of Prehistoric and Protohistoric Sciences (IUPPS) meetings to be held that year in Southampton. The convener of the conference was Peter Ucko, by then professor of archaeology at the University of Southampton. The symposium generated considerable controversy over the decision to exclude South African participants. The IUPPS withdrew its support, and the conference organizers decided to carry on without their involvement. Instead of just participating in the conference, I became one of the session organizers. A new world body for archaeology, the World Archaeological Congress (WAC), arose out of the conflict. It had a more radical stance than the IUPPS, recognizing that archaeology could not be seen as entirely separate from global political processes.

WAC aimed to widen the engagement of archaeology with cultures and societies outside the West and to include people from local regions and communities in the development of policy, and in influencing the objectives and methodologies of research. WAC was sensitive to the concerns of Native American activists about the curation of human remains and significant artefacts in museum collections and supported the passing of the Native American Graves Protection and Repatriation Act (NAGPRA) in 1990.[1] NAGPRA enables the repatriation of human remains to Native American communities with whom an identifiable connection has been established. The communities themselves can then decide on the treatment of the remains, ranging from reburial to continued holding in a museum collection. The repatriation of human remains had long been an important issue in Australia for some Aboriginal communities and their descendants.

At the Pitt Rivers Museum, I became involved in the issue of the repatriation of skeletal remains. The museum housed human remains from archaeological contexts in Britain and Europe but relatively few from elsewhere, except some that had been made into cultural artefacts – for example, drinking vessels, weapons, or religious artefacts. The museum's collection did, however, contain six skulls from Australia. The Australian government had just begun to develop processes for the repatriation of material from overseas institutions, facilitated by the National Museum of Australia. The Pitt Rivers Museum under Director Schuyler Jones became one of the first overseas museums to enter into positive discussions with Indigenous Australian representatives. In 1990, we were visited by two Australian Aboriginal leaders who had come to Britain to discuss the issue. They were Michael Mansell, an Indigenous Tasmanian lawyer, and Bob Weatherall, a Gamilaraay and Gemba man from the Foundation for Aboriginal and Islander Research Action in Queensland. The museum was requested to return the skulls to Australia, and the five that had known locations were repatriated by way of the National Museum of Australia. One remains in the museum's collection waiting to be identified.

In order to return human remains, the Pitt Rivers Museum had originally thought it might be necessary to change its statutes. In common with the ethical practice and responsibility of museums for their collections, strict conditions applied to the de-accessioning of objects. I was involved in discussions, with others, to change the museum's statutes to enable the de-accessioning of material in order return objects to source communities in particular circumstances. However, in the end, it was decided that the return could be made without requiring changes. I was subsequently involved in more general discussions of the issue with representatives of other museums as part of a process that would eventually result in a change to the Human Tissue Act 2004, s.47, which enabled de-accessioning of certain categories of human remains from a scheduled list of national institutions. Jenkins (2011: 47ff.) sees museum professionals' concern for the repatriation of human remains as having the potential to weaken the museum's duty of care for its collections. She concludes, 'There are significant internal influences from sector professionals who have focussed on this problem as a vehicle through which the authority of the museum can be challenged' (2011: 141). Arguably, the initiatives that we undertook in advance of any legislative requirement are an example.

I have some sympathy for Jenkins's view: there is a danger in museums responding too readily to external pressures to de-accession collections without reflecting deeply on their own value trajectory and on the history and considered decision-making processes that underlie their own practice. Jenkins's concern is for the slippery slope in which changes in museum practice open up and undermine the curation of collections in ways that make them less available for future generations of museum visitors and researchers. But Jenkins sees the response to requests for repatriation as a crisis of cultural authority, whereas I see these developments as being more in continuity with the trajectory of museum theory and practice, which has for some time been consciously and cautiously moving towards greater engagement with source communities. I see the process as developing within the museum community in response to the concerns of some source communities. People not working on collections have largely led the critique of museums and have indeed been at the forefront of challenging their cultural authority. In doing so, they have failed to recognize the agency of those working in and committed to museums in all their diversity who have responded in positive ways to concerns expressed by source communities.

***

In 1997, I left England to return to the ANU. The main project, which I still hope to complete, was to write a biography of the great Yolngu artist Narritjin Maymuru, but I became entangled, inevitably, with the core contemporary concerns of Yolngu.

When I returned to Yirrkala, a new crisis had developed over ambiguities in the Aboriginal Land Rights (Northern Territory) Act 1976 (ALR(NT)A). The act granted Yolngu the ownership of their land down to the low watermark. But what was the case when the tide came in? The Federal and Northern Territory governments acted as if the waters of the intertidal zone were not owned; hence, licences could be granted for crabbers and commercial fishermen, and sports fishing could carry on without permission of the landowners. Yolngu were troubled by the incursion onto their sea country and were deeply distressed when the severed head of a crocodile was left at an illegal campsite on land sacred to the ancestral Bäru (Crocodile) at Yatikpa in Blue Mud Bay.

The Yolngu response again gave art and material culture a central place in the campaign for justice. Yolngu artists made a set of 50 bark paintings, the *Saltwater* paintings, that, eventually, after touring venues across Australia, were acquired by the Australian National Maritime Museum in Sydney. The paintings mapped the shoreline under dispute, using the sacred patterns (*miny'tji*) that demonstrated Yolngu ownership of the intertidal zone. Yolngu also worked collaboratively with the National Museum of Australia to create 'Yingapungapu', one of the exhibitions for its opening in 2001 (Morphy 2006). A *yingapungapu* ceremony is associated with mortuary rituals. It centres on an elliptical sand sculpture created by ancestral women at a number of different locations in the north of Blue Mud Bay.

Yolngu viewed the paintings and the exhibitions as a way of demonstrating their concern and asserting their rights. But, as with the Bark Petition, the legal battle still had to be fought and won. The Northern Land Council, acting on behalf of the Yolngu, mounted a claim to the intertidal waters and lands of the northern part of Blue Mud Bay. Frances Morphy and I became involved in the case, which was heard under both the Native Title Act (Cth) 1993 and the ALR(NT)A.

The evidence in the hearings covered much of the ground prepared by the *Saltwater* paintings and the *Yingapungapu* exhibition. The ancestral *yingapungapu* ground was visited, and references to paintings were included in witness statements. Much of the evidence came from museums and archives stretching back to the first recorded encounter with British colonists – a meeting between Matthew Flinders and Yolngu in 1803.

The case was finally settled in favour of the Yolngu by the High Court of Australia in 2007, which in a majority decision recognized their ownership of the intertidal zone whether the tide was in or out. Art continued to be an effective way for Yolngu to act in the world.

***

And then back to the British Museum. For a number of years, I have been working with colleagues from the National Museum of Australia, the ANU, and the British Museum on a series of collaborative projects. The British Museum has one of the most important collections of Australian Aboriginal and Torres Strait Islander material culture, including many unique objects from the early years of European colonization. I had worked on some parts of the collection when I was a research assistant and later assisted in adding to the collections with paintings from Arnhem Land and central Australia. The first project focussed on the documentation of the collections and determining, where possible, the history of their manufacture and collection. Our aim was to trace their journey into the museum and establish a basis of connection to the communities from whence they came. At the conclusion of the project, we planned to organize two exhibitions as an outcome of the research, one in London and the other in Canberra.

We received exceptional support from the museums and from the Indigenous communities in Australia that we worked with. The project raised contentious issues, in particular that of the 'return to country' of significant objects from overseas collections. The lead curator for the exhibition in the British Museum was the Indigenous Tasmanian anthropologist Dr Gaye Sculthorpe and the title of the exhibition *Indigenous Australia Enduring Civilisation*.[2]

Notes

1 Williams (2013: 78) provides a succinct analysis of NAGPRA: 'These five statutes provide a portal into the interaction of archaeology as a profession and the national legislation promulgated by the US government. A meta-analysis of the five legislative acts would suggest that the dual policies of conservation and stewardship migrated from an uncontested position of all importance to one of great importance tempered with cultural empathy. Along with the documented migration, one can fairly characterize a fundamental change in the role of archaeologists from the star of the narrative to an important element in a sea of relationships surrounding the archaeological record' (https://lra.le.ac.uk/bitstream/2381/28187/1/2013WilliamsJFPhD.pdf).

2 In responding to my comments on an article she had written, Helena Robinson (2017: 902) wrote that 'Morphy's critique of my paper is written from the perspective of an insider deeply involved in the research that underpinned the related *Enduring Civilisation* exhibition, staged by the BM in London prior to the opening of Encounters'. This forward is in part an acknowledgement of the fact that my own history of involvement with museums and exhibitions has influenced my attitude to and understanding of them.

References

Fenton, J. (1982) "The Pitt Rivers Museum, Oxford," in *The Memory of War*, Edinburgh: Salamander Press.

Jenkins, T. (2011) *Contesting Human Remains in Museum Collections: The Crisis of Cultural Authority*, Abingdon: Routledge.

Jones, P. and Sutton, P. (1986) *Art and Land: Aboriginal Sculptures of the Lake Eyre Basin*, Adelaide: South Australian Museum in association with Wakefield Press.

Morphy, H. (1977) "Schematisation, meaning and communication in *toas*," in Ucko, P.J. (ed) *Form in Indigenous Art*, pp. 77–89, London: Duckworth.

Morphy, H. (2006) "Sites of persuasion: Yingapungapu at National Museum of Australia," in Karp, I., Kratz, C., Swatja, L. and Ybarra-Frausto, T. (eds) *Museum Frictions: Public Cultures/Global Transformations*, pp. 469–496, Durham, NC: Duke University Press.

Robinson, H. (2017) "Encountering complexity: debates around cultural democracy and participation," *International Journal of Heritage Studies*, 23 (9): 899–903.

Williams, J. (2013) *Archaeological Ethics in Armed Conflicts*, Unpublished PhD dissertation, University of Leicester.

2 Museums, ethnographic collections, and the creation of value

This book centres on the values associated with objects housed in museum collections and on the issues of rights in, and access to, those collections. I will argue that the two are closely related. My focus is on value creation associated with collections that in the past have been labelled 'ethnographic' and on the relationships between museums and the collections' source communities.

The determination of rights in museum objects often involves a struggle over value; it is not simply about whose rights need to be taken into account but about what kinds of value need to be respected in the formulation of those rights. The conceptual issue is complicated by the fact that the museums themselves are central players in value-creation processes; the value of their collections is subject to an almost continual process of change in which objects are understood and valued in new ways. In the case of cultural collections, the source communities are equally entangled in these value-creation processes; the curation, contextualization, and display of museum objects reflect how the source communities are viewed, valued, and understood. Value creation is a two-way process, and in the contemporary context, when both museum curators and representatives of source communities are in some respects co-present, the possibility of conflict, as well as collaboration, is ever present. The attitudes prevailing in the museum and source communities can be subject to quite different forces, and this may inhibit them in working together. My argument will not differentiate in too radical a way between the interests of these communities nor will it privilege one ontological perspective over the other. In my experience, the more museum and source communities collaborate, the more they see the utility of each other's methods and motives. They are, after all, collaborating in the production of value.

Museum collections always point in more than one direction, and they cross-cut time. From the perspective of value creation, they provide a vital source of information both on the societies that produced them and on the society of the collector at the time of collection (Bolton 2009). They enable understanding on a comparative basis, illuminating where contradiction and conflict arises, where boundaries can be crossed. Museums, viewed over time, provide evidence of processes of value transformation and category change within Western society. Value-creation processes within the museums' host society are central to the history and development of all museums. Museums need to persuade the visiting publics from their host communities that they are worthy of support because they contain things of value.

A wide range of factors come into play in shaping a society's attitudes to its museums and collections. Government policy, ideology, and budgetary concerns can have a major impact on cultural institutions; technological change and competing forms of entertainment can have an effect on museum audiences and their expectations; curatorial practices change over time, and attitudes and changing theories about the history and practice of museums are part of academic process.

While museums respond to change and are often at its forefront, they also need at times to be able to step aside from the process to preserve their core functions. The ideology of museums, their raison d'être, is that the value of the collections lies as much in their future potential as in their present use and past significance. Museums have a greater commitment to an idea of infinity than most other institutions because their value lies in the collections. Hence changes in policies and attitudes that threaten the integrity of the collections and their long-term curation – through dispersal, sale, or return – have the potential to transform them beyond recognition. Their ideology can be framed as conservative but in reality, at least from the perspective of the institution, it is more about conserving a resource that opens up an infinity of future possibilities for innovation and change in practice, research, and education.

The distinctiveness of ethnographic collections

This book is not primarily about the history of collections (see e.g. O'Hanlon and Welsch 2000), but it is important to reflect briefly on what is distinctive about ethnographic collections and why they have played such an important role in the recent history of museums. Museums and their collections are complex entities which are relatively autonomous of the processes of their creation and which provide a rich resource for recursive and reflexive practice. While making collections, curating objects, and handing them on from generation to generation is widespread in human history, the origins of the museum as a particular kind of cultural institution can be traced to the European Enlightenment and to the cabinets of curiosity of the preceding era. Ethnographic collections primarily comprise the material culture of the cultures and societies outside Europe encountered through trade in the process of colonial expansion. Initially, collections were made by missionaries, traders, military expeditions, explorers, colonial officials, and administrators. Worlds' Fairs and international exhibitions became another major source for ethnographic collections. They were subsequently followed by those whose scientific and humanistic interests developed in part out of contact with the collections themselves.

Over time, the collections have been used in fundamentally different ways, and their significance and value have changed. Ethnographic collections have been built over centuries. In the same period, the disciplines that study them have emerged, become differentiated, and undergone many transformations. Anthropology emerged as a distinctive discipline in the second half of the nineteenth century. Material culture became an important source of data for anthropological research and systematic fieldwork-based collections began to be made. Ethnology was one of those sets of terms that eventually became subsumed under the broader rubric of anthropology as the study of 'people, culture, and society'. Ethnography is the method of first-hand recording of data, developed as the preferred method of research.

The collections of the major ethnographic museums, thus, have very mixed origins, and their diverse backgrounds are reflected in the nature of the documentation that accompanies them. The eighteenth century voyages of discovery in the Pacific under Cook, Vancouver, and others involved the systematic collection of material culture as part of the process of documenting the resources of the regions they visited. While, subsequently, many of those collections were dispersed and the documentation lost, others, such as those made by Johann and George Forster, remained largely intact (Hetherington and Morphy 2009). The Forsters gave over 200 artefacts from the Pacific to the University of Oxford, accompanied by a systematic catalogue. Today, they are part of the collection at the Pitt Rivers Museum. A second collection of 300 artefacts collected by them and purchased from Johann's widow is held in the Georg-August Museum in Göttingen. However, most of the early collections were acquired from secondary sources through auction houses, gifts from individuals or their estates, dealers in ethnographic curios, and so on. Museums and their curators were disconnected from the makers of the collections – the source communities – and detailed contextual knowledge was not their primary concern. The earliest collections were built in an era before the emergence of anthropology as a discipline, and yet they were integral to the process of its development.

Anthropology developed in the nineteenth century in an environment in which museums, evolving out of cabinets of curiosity and the encyclopaedic imagination of the Enlightenment, were an integral part of European intellectual discourse. In universities such as Oxford, anthropology first found its place in the museum and only later on moved into an academic department. Anthropology was one of a cluster of embryonic disciplines that developed grand comparative schema for the history and evolution of human society. In the second part of the nineteenth century, evolutionary theory was the dominant paradigm in the natural sciences and became an important theme of discourse in anthropology. Museum collections were used as a resource for demonstrating evolutionary sequences over time and identifying formal series that were presumed to provide insights into the origins of things. Researchers were motivated both by their reflection on and curiosity about the European past, known largely from its material remains, and a complementary interest in the different lives of people in the present. The two interests were often entangled. The researchers saw evidence of their own past in ghostly survivals of the folklore and customs of a 'bygone' era (Hoyt 2001). They also saw their past in the practices of non-European and often colonized societies that fitted into analogous places in imagined evolutionary hierarchies. Data from the diversity of world societies was used as evidence for possible evolutionary sequences from earlier forms of human society to those represented by modern Western society – a move from barbarism to classical civilization and its continuing traditions.

Anthropology's focus for most of the nineteenth century remained outside the European present. The dominant evolutionary paradigm ordered societies on the basis of the presumed complexity of their technological systems and social organization. Analogies were drawn between different societies and early stages of the development of European societies. In Europe, some ethnographic museums, including the British Museum and the Pitt Rivers Museum, also collected their 'own' regional material culture, the culture of European 'times past', which in America became the subject of folklore museums. Such materials are an often forgotten, but important, component of ethnographic collections that can challenge some of the preconceptions about the category as it changed over time. The material culture of everyday life, the musical and oral traditions that fitted into the category of folklore were frequently devalued by cosmopolitan society but not by the collectors themselves. The collectors too were motivated by a desire to collect objects and bodies of knowledge that they were afraid would otherwise be lost and conserve them as a resource for the future when their value would be better appreciated.

The characteristic of ethnographic collections made in the nineteenth and early twentieth centuries were their comprehensive nature. The intention was to collect objects that represented the lives of the source communities and ideally to provide accompanying documentation that enabled them to be placed in the context of their use and significance. The main bias of collection was towards material culture that was as little modified as possible by the impact of colonization.[1]

While some well-documented collections were made earlier by missionaries and colonial officials, the majority of well-documented collections date from the very end of the nineteenth century when anthropology had developed as a fieldwork-based discipline. The major collections made by anthropologists such as Spencer and Gillen, Haddon, Boas, and Mason had few earlier equivalents.[2] The collections tended to be eclectic and not bound to established categories or typologies except at the most general level. While typological methods were employed to understand the relationships between objects, they did not determine what was collected. Certain objects became fashionable for a while, and certain items became desired if not essential components of a representative collection. Museums and individual collectors often made an effort to collect multiple examples of the same object, both for methodological reasons and in order to exchange material with other museums often on an international basis.

The ethnographic turn

David Hoyt (2001) argues persuasively that the end of the nineteenth century marked a major transformation in anthropology. The focus began to move towards ethnography – to studying living societies in depth. The key method of anthropology became the first-hand recording of data based on fieldwork and participant observation. Hoyt (2001: 332) quotes the French anthropologist van Gennep:

> If the nineteenth century was the century of the historical sciences, then the twentieth was to be that of the ethnographical sciences . . . ethnography in the twentieth century will be the foundation upon which a new conception of mankind will be constructed.[3]

The emphasis on ethnography was partly because it was realized that the existing data was inadequate both for comparative analysis in the present and for the historical reconstruction of the past. Anthropology began to emerge in its present form through the rejection of speculative history and through an emphasis on the quality of its data. The rejection of simplistic social evolutionary perspectives that had been challenged on the basis of existing data was a complementary factor that supported the shift of focus to understanding living societies on their own terms.

The idea that some contemporary societies could be seen as evolutionarily prior to others had indeed been problematized quite early on in the emergence of anthropology as an academic discipline. Museum anthropology was an integral component of the challenge to its theoretical dominance. As Wintle (2015: 1496) writes,

> Shifts in U.S. museum practice across the twentieth century were driven by a number of important factors: in the last years of the nineteenth century, the anthropologist Franz Boas had already made persuasive arguments discrediting the evolutionary display paradigm.

In Britain, Haddon was moving to a position critical of race-based evolutionism,[4] and Baldwin Spencer's writings on Australian Aboriginal society, though frequently asserted to be framed by Fraser's evolutionism, largely failed to support his theories (Urry 1972: 49; Morphy 2015).

The evolutionist theories of the nineteenth century as applied to contemporary societies had been challenged both on theoretical grounds and by accumulated evidence. The move to fieldwork-based research was relatively independent of that change and was determined by multiple factors. One factor was the belief that it was only through long-term research and detailed participant observation that reliable, testable data could be obtained. The environment for undertaking research was facilitated by the relative stability brought about by colonial control, and there was a belief, albeit much contested, that anthropology could be of benefit to the administration of colonies by facilitating better understanding of the colonized societies.[5] But the motivations involved in the development of anthropology were multiple, and arguably, the main motivation for many was the intrinsic interest in understanding different ways of being human and in the appreciation of cultural diversity.

The changing focus to studying societies in their own terms resulted in a shift in the theoretical focus of social and cultural anthropology. It is often referred to as a paradigm change from evolutionism to structural-functionalism, but this fails to capture the diversity of theoretical perspectives at play. The twentieth century became one of disciplinary differentiation in which disciplines which at one time had shared a family resemblance – anthropology, sociology, psychology, history, art history, geography – began to consciously define their own fields and boundaries, partly in opposition to one another.

The priority that anthropology gave to ethnography – studying society as it existed in the present on the basis of direct observation of behaviour – lessened the focus on history and change. And, ironically perhaps, that determination to focus on the particular societies as a precursor to comparative analysis meant that in anthropologist's writings, if not in their fieldnotes, societies were presented as if they existed independent of the colonial context in which they were embedded. Certainly, there was greater emphasis on small-scale societies relatively unaffected by colonization, but not an exclusive one. The emphasis on the quality, reliability, and objectivity of the data obtained through fieldwork meant that anthropologists did establish close relationships with the people they were studying – it was arguably a requirement of the method. And that closeness often set them at odds with members of their own society – 'difficult folk' as Mills refers to them in the title of his book on the history of the discipline.

Hoyt (2001: 334) summarizes the change of direction of anthropology at the turn of the twentieth century elegantly when he writes,

> The primitive entered Victorian ethnographic discourse as a *revenant*, a visitor from the dead summoned by the ethnographic medium, and passed into the twentieth century transformed from an apparition into an agent, if still a heavily restrained and guarded one.

And, arguably, it is that process of acknowledgement of agency and the subsequent closing of distance between observer and observed that characterizes the trajectory of anthropology in the twentieth and twenty-first century leading to 'a redistribution of the economy of agency' (Hoyt 2001: 350).

The revulsion felt by later anthropologists over race-based evolutionary theories influenced the way the discipline would approach historical and comparative projects for a considerable time and continues to cause tensions within the discipline as whole. While archaeology continues to focus on the longue duré and biological anthropology is at the centre of studies of human evolution, social and cultural anthropologists still feel a reluctance in becoming part of the whole. Any theory that threatens to place contemporary human societies into temporal sequences by positioning them in the past has to be treated with caution. The use of ethnographic parallels in archaeological research is a good area to focus on to tune in to this discomfort. On the one hand, many archaeologists opt for the purity of science, and on the other hand, many cultural anthropologists remain reluctant to use data from contemporary societies in order to understand the past. And this discomfort is reinforced by the fact that people outside the discipline seem to delight in positioning anthropology in their own colonial past rather than as being at the forefront of the critique of race-based theories.

Anthropology's move away from museums

The neglect of material culture, museums, and archives in anthropology characterized much of twentieth century anthropology. The lack of interest in part contributed to an emerging orthodoxy in which museums became associated with anthropology's past, both in theoretical terms and through their entanglement with colonialism. Museum collections were viewed in part as symptoms of a colonial heritage, filled with trophies appropriated from Indigenous cultures (Jordanova 1989). The critical gaze directed towards ethnographic museums and the history of collections has been productive in the broader arena of theoretical discourse on colonialism and government. Ethnographic museums entered critical discourse as exemplars of an exhibitionary complex (Bennett 1995), which in the late nineteenth century operated to order peoples into developmental sequence, leading to the then present. Under that Foucauldian framework, collections and the ways in which they were exhibited and presented are seen as integral to the process of governance through regulating the behaviour and influencing the values of the museum public.

While there are elements of truth in such framings, they fail to recognize the particularities of the different collections, the changes in museum practices over time, the research potential of collections for uncovering forgotten histories, and, perhaps most important of all, neglecting to consider the agency of the people who cooperated to make the collections – the Indigenous makers and the colonial collectors. While the building of ethnographic collections articulated with colonial processes – many of the collectors were the government officials and missionaries who occupied the frontier – the collectors were often among the few to engage positively with Indigenous populations and attempt to challenge or slow down the colonial process (see Cole 1991).

As Jonaitis and Glass (2010: 8) argue,

> Colonial encounters were not strictly dualistic phenomena with Euroamericans oppressing and native people succumbing. . . . Native people often became active participants who over several hundred years, engaged responded to and negotiated with their colonizers.

Museums with ethnography

Ethnographic collections are housed in many different kinds of museums. They may have been built up as part of major national museums of culture – the so-called encyclopaedic museums – such as the British Museum, or included in the collections of natural history museums, as in New York and Washington, DC. In other cases, such as the Pitt Rivers Museum, they are the core collections of museums of anthropology. The National Museum of the American Indian in Washington, DC, and New York was built on the Native American collections of George Gustav Hey. Some combinations appear at first to be surprising. The Auckland War Memorial Museum has sections devoted to the nation's war dead and the history of New Zealand's engagement in external warfare and natural history, as well as holding important Maori and Pacific Island sections. The Autry Museum of the American West in Los Angeles combines America's 'Western' heritage with one of the most important collections of Native American art and material culture, acquired when it incorporated the Southwest Museum of the American Indian Collection.[6] In recent years, in a move that signals the challenge to simplistic categorizations of institutions, works from ethnographic collections are increasingly being exhibited in art museums.

There are substantial ethnographic collections in most of the regional museums across the British Isles and in many European countries. Museums in cities such as Brighton, Belfast, Edinburgh, Glasgow, Manchester, and Plymouth have their own variously named ethnographic collections. The museum in the small town of Stromness in the Orkney Islands, one of the oldest museums in the British Isles, has significant objects from the Pacific and North America, some acquired in the eighteenth century. Stromness was the last watering place for ships of the Hudson Bay Company en route to North America between 1670 and 1891, and for Cook's vessels *Resolution* and *Discovery* in 1780.

The framings of ethnographic collections and the museums which house them are the products of such diverse histories that any categorization is a simplification and, as it turns out, usually only provisional. The British Museum was founded in 1753 with the gift of Sir Hans Sloane's 'cabinet of curiosities' to the nation. The ethnographic collections subsequently became part of the Museum's Antiquities Department before the establishment of the Department of Ethnography as late as 1946. Between 1970 and 1997, the department became the Museum of Mankind, housed in Burlington Gardens, before taking its present name as the Department of Africa, Oceania, and the Americas in 2004. And as the names changed, so did the contents of the institutions. European and Asian collections, which were once included in the Ethnography Department are no longer there. The Department of Oriental Antiquities became Asia, the Ancient Near East has become the Middle East, and, in both cases, the departments' collections have been enlarged by material culture previously housed in the Ethnography Department. And British and European ethnography became part of the Department of Britain, Europe, and Prehistory, established in 2003. Perhaps all museum collections have an agglomerative aspect since they inevitably contain more of interest and value than institutional names divisions and labels can ever represent.

Ethnographic collections are both uncomfortable and comfortable in their different locations, depending on how they are framed and interpreted. The changing names and fuzzy boundaries are indicators of histories. Words gain meaning in the present that they did not have in the past. And, just as significantly, the public of the host society radically changes its understanding of the world and the relationships between people in the present, in the past, and over time. Antiquities, antiquarians, and antiques have connotations that distance many of the collections from how they are seen today and the value that they have.

Ethnography is a word that, in the museum world, comes with connotations of a past disciplinary history associated with the development of anthropology as a discipline, with evolutionism and its critiques, and the methods of participant observation. The relationships between academic disciplines, the subjects of their research, the methods employed, and the theories developed are disjunctive, often discontinuous, but always have the potential for recursivity – for going back to reconsider relationships with the passage of time. Participant observation – fieldwork – was closely associated with the building of museum collections through Boas, Haddon and Spencer, and Gillen. But soon after, in the first quarter of the twentieth century, anthropologists moved away from material culture.

The collections were no less valuable, but for a time, they were no longer central to anthropological research and in a sense were curated and conserved to await a time they would be valued again in different ways. Museums played an important role in maintaining the links between the fractured fields of anthropology. Ethnographic collections and archaeological collections tend to be housed in the same institutions and managed, if sometimes uncomfortably, as related collections.

During its period of near exile from social anthropology, museum anthropology embraced new technologies; it was where visual anthropology developed, where photographic collections were housed, where some anthropologists' archives found a home. And the engagement today continues with developments in digital technology. Ethnographic museums had a continuing relationship with the Western art worlds; with contemporary art practice; with collectors of the arts of Asia, Oceania, Africa, and the Americas; and with a public interested in what was referred to as 'primitive' art. The relationship with the fine art worlds began to have a strong edge to it. Anthropologists on the whole were intolerant of the idea of primitivism and the implicit categorization of societies as primitive; they were cautious of employing art as a cross-cultural category and highly conflicted over the market in 'primitive' art. The essential relativism of anthropology makes anthropologists suspicious of making qualitative judgements. Yet at the same time, in settler-colonial societies, from the USA to Australia, museum anthropologists were beginning to play a role in the marketing of Indigenous arts and asserting its continuing and contemporary existence.

A return to the museum

The past half-century has seen a transformation in the theory and practice of museum anthropology. As a result, ethnographic collections are moving gradually to the centre of theoretical discourse in anthropology. The changes have occurred in two broad domains. Museum anthropology was centrally involved in the reflexive turn in anthropology, in which the history of the discipline and its representational practices came under a critical review (Clifford 1997). The other major change has been in the relationships between researchers, museums, and what are often referred to as source communities – the people who made or make the objects that comprise the collections and their descendants. These domains are connected, in that both involve attempts to close the distance between anthropologists and the subjects of their research in the context of a complex history of engagement.

Anthropology as a discipline has played a central and at times controversial role in cross-cultural understanding and has inevitably become entangled in colonial and postcolonial processes. While for much of its history the primary audience for anthropology has been a Euro-American one – explaining the Other to a Western Us – at the local level, anthropologists have always been involved in much more dialogical relationships. In an increasingly interconnected world, anthropology has become a more global discipline, and a change in the conceptualization and value of ethnographic collections has been part of that process. The globalization of museum practice requires a coincidence of interests that facilitates access to and use of collections but acknowledges fundamental differences in how they are seen and conceptualized by different audiences.

Much of the recent theoretical engagement of anthropology with museum collections has concerned the history of collections, the relationships they entail, and the role museums and collections have played in discourse about culture. Researchers have been tracing the social life of things (Appadurai 1986) and have recognized the entanglement of material culture and collecting in colonial processes (Thomas 1991). They have seen museums positioned critically as zones of contact (Clifford 1997). In the case of the Pitt Rivers Museum, curators developed the concept of the relational museum in which collections are connected to individuals and communities in different ways (Gosden and Larson 2007). There has been increased recognition of the important role trade played in the building of collections and indigenous cultural production (Graburn 1976; Myers 2001), which in turn has problematized simplistic concepts of authenticity (Morphy 2007; Jonaitis and Glass 2010).

The theoretical discourse surrounding museums and ethnographic collections has resulted in changes in museum practice. In particular, museums in settler-colonial countries' societies have had an increasing history of engagement with local Indigenous populations (Ames 1992; Tapsell 2000; Morphy 2006; Isaac 2007; Leopold 2013). In a seminal series of co-edited volumes, Ivan Karp played a major role in moving museums and their collections back to the centre stage of anthropology by re-integrating them into the contemporary concerns of the discipline (Karp and Lavine 1991; Karp et al. 1992; Karp et al. 2006). Karp saw better than anyone else the complex network of entanglement that connects museums and anthropology, operating in the domain of public culture, to global processes. As he and Cory Kratz wrote in their magisterial introduction to *Museum Frictions*, 'At once facing inward to local constituencies and outward to wider audiences . . . [museums] . . . have become essential forms through which to make statements about history, identity, value, and place and to claim recognition' (Karp and Kratz 2006: 4).

In developing their insight, we can say that ethnographic museums are sites of added complexity because they contain two locals: the local of the museum and its immediate audience and the displaced local of the source community where objects originated. In recent years, those two locals have come together, often needing to repair a spatio-temporal disjunction. The relationship between the two locals – the Indigenous communities and the museums that house their collections – is characterized by discontinuities over time that vary according to the history and impact of European colonization. Societies that were colonized early on have often undergone centuries of separation from their collections in the museum. Very often, the populations suffered decline as a result of dispossession, violence, and disease, and local production was disrupted by policies of colonial governments or missionary organizations that discouraged or banned traditional practices, alienated people from their land, and disrupted processes of knowledge transmission.

The materiality of collections

The value of museum collections lies to a great extent in their materiality. They comprise objects preserved from the past that can continually be re-examined, recontextualized, and brought into the present. In a postcolonial world, the relevance of anthropology has changed and so too in many respects have the topics of its research. The contents of ethnographic collections, however, have largely remained in place. They are as much from the past as they are in the present. The present crisis in museums is created in part because in recent times, they have taken on new and often emotionally charged roles. They too have changed and are changing, despite in some respects maintaining a visceral connection to past times. The very materiality of collections, the immediacy of the connection to the past, and the obligation to give people access to them and to exhibit them to wider publics makes museums an ideal venue for raising uncomfortable issues.

In containing the material evidence of past times, collections contain objects that bring to mind the life of the maker, perhaps even more than photographs do. Ethnographic collections connect source communities deeply in positive and negative ways to their histories. But just as importantly, they bring the European and colonial American past into the present by the buildings they occupy and by the duty of the institution to preserve their past through labels, catalogues, and documentation.[7]

The primary responsibility of museums to store, catalogue, and conserve their collections creates an enduring link with the past and places constraints on the process of change. The British Museum, completed in 1852, with its powerful columnated entrance conjoining classical civilization with imperial power, and the Pitt Rivers Museum, built in 1886 like a huge industrial engine-shed, reflect different aspects of the Victorian era, which they straddle. Inevitably, they become symbols of a past era when the British Empire reached its apotheosis. At the same time they are buildings that are hard to replace or displace, both because they are designed to house vast collections and have become, in their own right, culturally significant objects. The pressure may be on downsizing the collections and making the buildings into something else – venues for travelling exhibitions, forums for discussion. It appears at times as if the cultural significance of collections lies solely in their value as heritage – locking them into time and history.

The Pitt Rivers Museum, often portrayed as an embodiment of typological classification, assiduously revises its labels and exhibitions to remove implications of evolutionary progress from lower to higher forms of society. The collections are redisplayed, bringing new sets of objects together to show different relationships and present new information. The podcasts, sound guides, and web resources take interpretation in many directions, often challenging past assumptions. The Pitt Rivers Museum tries to escape the negative part of its heritage. But for some, the very effort it makes and its diligence in maintaining records of past typologies and terminologies keeps the past alive.

Conclusion: ethnographic collections and the creation of value

Ethnographic collections and the museums that hold and curate them have played a central role in the value-creation processes that have changed attitudes towards race and cultural difference and made people (museum visitors) aware of the richness and variety of human history. They exist at the ever-changing point of articulation between the source communities (the cultures of production), and the people and cultures of the museum as a predominantly Western institution. Museum collections and the associated archives provide the resources for entering those periods of history when colonial encounters and expanding trade relationships transformed people's lives. The collections carry traces of tragic and unconscionable encounters at the same time as they reveal the richness of past and contemporary cultures.

In the history of colonization, museums were both in step with colonial processes that facilitated the building of collections and ahead of them. They challenged theories based on race and recognized the value of cultural diversity. The collections played and continue to play a significant role in demonstrating the value and richness of *other* ways of life and in initiating slow processes of change in the domain of human rights, challenging received hierarchies, and changing the meaning of terms from the past (Sculthorpe 2015).

Presentist views provide a block to understanding the complexity of historical processes because they impose a uniformitarian view on the past and fail to account for people's agency in working towards a future which at the time they could only partly imagine. If we make assumptions about the motivations of the producers and collectors on the basis of what we know happened subsequent to their time, we distance them from ourselves without understanding the role they played in the process of change that led to where we are now.

Notes

1 The objects themselves, however, have become an important source for understanding the change and impact of colonization both in material terms and in the nature of the relationships that developed (Thomas 1991).

2 Hans Vermeulen (2015) argues that Boasian anthropology comes out of a longer history of fieldwork-based anthropology in central and eastern Europe that can be traced back to the late eighteenth century.

3 Hoyt's (2001: 332) citation comes from Arnold van Gennep's *Titres at Travaux* (1911), as cited in Nicole Belmont, *Arnold Gennep: The Creator of French Ethnography*, translated by Derek Coltman (Chicago, 1979), 115.

4 Huxley and Haddon (1935: 107) argued that 'the term *race* as applied to human groups should be dropped from the vocabulary of science' because 'migration and crossing have produced such a fluid state of affairs that no such clear-cut term, as applied to existing conditions, is permissible'.

5 Basu (2016), in his reappraisal of N.W. Thomas's work in Nigeria between 1909 and 1913, illustrates well the ambiguous role and limited agency of the government anthropologist in influencing the process and policy of colonial governance.

6 The Autry Museum provides a case study of the ways in which the shifting values of indigenous cultural material has the potential to make a difference in cultural

institutions. The Autry Museum has moved from being essentially a history of the colonial West, with an inevitable emphasis on the cowboy era, to becoming a broader history of the region. The rich Native American collections acquired through the 2003 incorporation of the collections of the Southwest Museum of the American Indian transformed the balance of the collections. In addition to giving a prominence to Native American history and its continuing presence in the region, the shift in emphasis allows the history of 'West' to be viewed in a different way. The 'West' as a story of invasion is no longer masked, but the 'West' as the origin of styles, musical traditions that influenced the history of cinema, and that played a central role in the development of cultural forms that indigenous people have engaged globally can also be acknowledged.

7 Harrison (1997: 46), for example, argues, 'The overarching "structure of containment" of these configurations was the museum buildings themselves, be it the ethnographic museums in Europe or the natural history museums in the United States. These buildings set apart the colonial subject from other aspects of the social world to which their material objects had been transported and affirmed them as "subjects" '.

References

Ames, M. (1992) *Cannibal Tours and Glass Boxes*, Vancouver: UBC Press.

Appadurai, A. (1986) *The Social Life of Things*, New York: New School University.

Basu, P. (2016) "N.W. Thomas and colonial anthropology in British West Africa: reappraising a cautionary tale," *Journal of the Royal Anthropological Institute*, (N.S.) 22: 84–107.

Belmont, N. (1979) *Arnold van Gennep: The Creator of French Ethnography*, translated by Derek Coltman, Chicago: University of Chicago Press.

Bennett, T. (1995) *The Birth of the Museum: History, Theory, Politics*, London and New York: Routledge.

Bolton, L. (2009) "Brushed with fame: museological investments in the Cook voyage collection," in Hetherington, M. and Morphy, H. (eds) *Discovering Cook's Collections*, Canberra: National Museum of Australia.

Clifford, J. (1997) "Museums as contact zones," in Clifford, J. (ed) *Routes: Travel and Translation in the Late Twentieth Century*, pp. 188–219, Cambridge, MA and London: Harvard University Press.

Cole, D. (1991) "Tricks of the trade: some reflections on anthropological collecting," *Arctic Anthropology*, 28 (1): 48–52.

Gosden, C. and Larson, F. (2007) *Knowing Things: Exploring Collections at the Pitt Rivers Museum 1884–1945*, Oxford: Oxford University Press.

Graburn, N. (1976) *Ethnic and Tourist Arts: Cultural Expressions from the Fourth World*, Berkeley: University of California Press.

Harrison, J. (1997) "Museums as agencies of neocolonialism in a postmodern world," *Studies in Cults, Organizations and Societies*, 3 (1): 41–65.

Hetherington, M. and Morphy, H. (eds) (2009) *Discovering Cook's Collections*, Canberra: National Museum of Australia Press.

Hoyt, D.L. (2001) "The reanimation of the primitive: fin-de-siècle ethnographic discourse in Western Europe," *History of Science*, 39 (3): 331–354.

Huxley, J. and Haddon, A.C. (1935) *We Europeans: A Survey of "Racial" Problems*, London: Jonathan Cape.

Isaac, G. (2007) *Mediating Knowledges: Origins of a Museum for the Zuni People*, Tucson: University of Arizona Press.

Jonaitis, A. and Glass, A. (2010) *The Totem Pole: An Intercultural History*, Washington: University of Washington Press.

Jordanova, L. (1989) "Objects of knowledge: a historical perspective on museums," in Vergo, P. (ed) *The New Museology*, pp. 22–41, London: Reaktion Books.

Karp, I. and Kratz, C. (2006) "Introduction: museum frictions," in Karp, I., Kratz, C., Szwaja, L. and Ybarra-Frausto, T. (eds) *Museum Frictions: Public Cultures/Global Transformations*, pp. 1–35, Durham, NC: Duke University Press.

Karp, I., Kratz, C., Szwaja, L. and Ybarra-Frausto, T. (eds) (2006) *Museum Frictions: Public Cultures/Global Transformations*, Durham, NC: Duke University Press.

Karp, I., Kreamer, C. and Lavine, S. (eds) (1992) *Museums and Communities: The Politics of Public Culture*, Washington: The Smithsonian Institution Press.

Karp, I. and Lavine, S.D. (1991) *Exhibiting Culture: The Poetics and Politics of Museum Display*, Washington: Smithsonian Institute Press.

Leopold, R. (2013) "Articulating culturally sensitive knowledge online: a Cherokee case study," *Museum Anthropology Review*, 7: 85–104.

Morphy, H. (2006) "Sites of persuasion: Yingapungapu at National Museum of Australia," in Karp, I., Kratz, C., Swatja, L. and Ybarra-Frausto, T. (eds) *Museum Frictions: Public Cultures/Global Transformations*, pp. 469–496, Durham, NC: Duke University Press.

Morphy, H. (2007) *Becoming Art: Exploring Cross-Cultural Categories*, Oxford: Berg.

Morphy, H. (2015) "Indigenous Australia: enduring civilisation, a personal reflection," *Museum Worlds: Advances in Research*, 3 (1): 7–17.

Morphy, H. (2017) "Encounters at the National Museum of Australia: a moment in an ongoing process of engagement," *International Journal of Heritage Studies*, 23 (9): 875–878.

Myers, F. (ed) (2001) *The Empire of Things: Regimes of Value and Material Culture*, Oxford: James Currey.

O'Hanlon, M. and Welsch, R.L. (eds) (2000) *Hunting the Gatherers: Ethnographic Collectors, Agents and Agency in Melanesia, 1870s-1930s*, pp. 1–34, Oxford: Berghahn.

Sculthorpe, G. (2015) "Caring for, conserving and storing human remains, part two: introduction," in Fletcher, A., Antoine, D. and Hill, J.D. (eds) *Regarding the Dead: Human Remains in the British Museum*, pp. 31–34, London: British Museum Press.

Tapsell, P. (2000) *Pukaki: A Comet Returns*, Auckland: Reed Publishing.

Thomas, N. (1991) *Entangled Objects: Exchange, Material Culture, and Colonialism in the Pacific*, Cambridge, MA: Harvard University Press.

Urry, J. (1972) "Notes & queries on anthropology and the development of field methods in British anthropology, 1870–1920 (Hocart prize essay)," *Proceedings of the Royal Anthropological Institute*, 45–57.

Vermeulen, H.F. (2015) *Before Boas: The Genesis of Ethnography and Ethnology in the German Enlightenment*, Lincoln: University of Nebraska Press.

Wintle, C. (2015) "Decolonizing the Smithsonian: museums as a microcosm of political encounter," *American Historical Review*, 121 (5): 1492–1521.

3 Different locals

Reflections on Indigenous Australian collections

The particular nature of the impact of colonial history is bound to affect how the descendants of the people who produced the objects in the collections view those collections and the institutions that house them. Addressing the relationship between museums' ethnographic collections and history of European colonization requires that the specificities of the relationships need to be addressed. This chapter will focus on two related topics: the role that museum anthropology and ethnographic collections have played in value-creation processes and the relationships that were involved in building the collections.

Australia provides an excellent case study for examining the dynamics of the relationships between the local of the Indigenous community and the institution of the museum over time. The time span of the colonial era also intersects crucially with the emergence of anthropology as a discipline.

There are great differences in the colonial histories of different regions of Australia that have resulted in very different relationships between source communities and museum collections. Australian Aboriginal and Torres Strait Islander collections have been built up since the beginning of the colonial encounter with British and French voyagers in the late eighteenth century. Artefacts from the first encounter between James Cook and the local people of Botany Bay ended up in the collections of the Cambridge Museum of Archaeology and Anthropology (Nugent, M. and Sculthorpe, G. 2018).

On the whole, the history of museum collections has been one of collecting at the frontier or excavating the past once the frontier had moved on (Peterson et al. 2008). The making of collections has always been entangled with the politics of the frontier, with the control of Indigenous people, and, until recently, with the appropriation of their land. There is considerable evidence that some objects in museum collections are there as a consequence of frontier violence. The British Museum holds a number of objects donated in the 1870s by John Ewen Davidson (1841–1923) a Scottish pioneer of the Queensland sugar industry. He wrote about an encounter where he and his partner shot and killed at least one Aboriginal person and noted, 'There was plenty of blood on one or two shields, which we picked up'.[1] A similar history is reflected in collections from other parts of Australia; Orde's collections from the Kimberley provide another example.

> [In] the arduous and unpleasant duty of arresting the blacks outback from Derby . . . I had managed to accumulate a number of native weapons and thought they might be of value and interest to the museum . . . the weapons are genuine native weapons of the type taken by the police from native camps.
>
> (Coates 2015: 168)

However, not all collections made on the frontier were covered with blood, and many of those who made the collections on the frontier were people who had a positive engagement with Aboriginal people, albeit in a colonial context. It was the positive nature of their relationships that enabled them to build substantial collections that, in retrospect, can be seen as collaborative processes. The nature of the relationship is also reflected in the documentation of the collections, which clearly shows that the collectors were interested in the objects they collected not as trophies but for the information they revealed about the people who made them. The people who contributed most significantly to museum collections in the latter part of the nineteenth century were missionaries, pastoralists, government officials, and professional people employed in regions after they had been 'settled' and the violence of the frontier had moved on.

Reversing the order

I had originally drafted this chapter in a chronological sequence, beginning with the building of anthropological collections in the nineteenth century and moving forward in time. However, I began to realize that for many reasons, such a linear view pulled against the argument that I wanted to make. Setting the earlier collections in the context of the colonial history of Australia positioned them as tightly anchored to the process of colonization. Instead, the history of collections complexifies the narrative of relations between colonizers and colonized, introducing a frame within which the agency of both sets of actors are significant factors. I also do this consciously to distance anthropology from the early period of Australian colonization. The discipline took shape in the later part of the nineteenth century and increasingly challenged European presuppositions about Australian Aboriginal society.

Although the impact of colonization differed greatly across Australia, the agency, and motivations of Indigenous Australians, as the frontier reached them, it seems to have been consistent. We can with hindsight see distinct similarities between the ways in which Gweagal people of Botany Bay approached the invaders of the First Fleet in 1788, and the way the Noongar interacted with Stirling in 1829, and how Yolngu people of eastern Arnhem Land confronted European intruders in the 1920s. Inga Clendinnen's evocative phrase 'dancing with strangers' (2005) hints at an attitude that cuts across place and time – an orientation towards engagement and inclusion. The history of colonization, from this perspective, can be seen as an ongoing value-creation process. Engagement with Indigenous Australians over time moved from moments of genocide to moments of inclusion. Indigenous Australians have played a fundamental role in shifting colonists' values and changing their attitudes, but they have done so from a position of limited power, and for most of European Australia's history, there has been virtually no acknowledgement of their agency.

For this reason, my initial focus in this chapter is not on the earlier stage of the building of anthropological collections but on a more recent history focussed on the Yolngu people of eastern Arnhem Land. The first mission stations were established in Arnhem Land in the 1920s, and major ethnographic collections and anthropological research began at the same time. I will argue that in many respects, the researchers were following the trajectory of their predecessors and engaged in the same kinds of value creation. However, in this case, the agency of the source communities can be more easily documented, both at the time of collection and through retrospective oral history.

My aim is not to deny the reality of the colonial process but to offer a more nuanced account which draws attention to the agency of Indigenous Australians and recognizes that those who built the collections were often those most supportive of Aboriginal causes. My aim is to look back from a recent past in which we have a fairly detailed history of the encounter to reflect on the motivations of the people who built earlier collections and who made the objects. In the long term, the argument can only build on evidence from the time the collections were made. The research into the history of collections and Indigenous agency at different moments in time is only just beginning, but I hope that the perspective I adopt will allow people to look for a different kind of evidence rather than just for evidence which links museums solely to the hegemonic process of colonialism.

My analysis centres on a particular aspect of the value-creation process – the recognition of the aesthetic attributes of Indigenous cultural production. This is an area in which it is possible to trace a trajectory of recognition which involved conceptual change and which led, over time, to the widespread recognition of Australian Aboriginal art within Australia and on a global basis. While this recognition does not in itself address present inequities or past oppression, it is an important step in acknowledging the coevalness of different cultures in a world of continuing diversity.

Making Yolngu collections

The Yolngu people of eastern Arnhem Land first came under Australian government control in the 1920s and 1930s with the establishment of mission stations established by the Methodist Overseas Mission at Milingimbi, Yirrkala, and Elcho Island (Galiwin'ku). From that time on, the Yolngu have produced art and material culture objects for sale (for details, see Morphy 2007). Many of these objects were sold through the mission stores or to the military, who were based in Arnhem Land during World War II. However, eastern Arnhem Land has also provided some of the major anthropological collections of art and material culture now housed in museums in Australia, the USA, and Europe. Lloyd Warner was the first anthropologist to make significant collections of Yolngu material culture when he conducted fieldwork at Milingimbi between 1927 and 1929.[2] Donald Thomson built his collection between 1935 and 1942, Ronald and Catherine Berndt made theirs in 1946, and Charles Mountford and the Australian-American Scientific Expedition to Arnhem Land made significant collections in 1948. Subsequently, major collections were made by other anthropologists, including Karel Kupka in the 1950s, Helen Groger-Wurm in the 1970s, and Howard and Frances Morphy in the 1970s. All these well-documented collections could be a resource for future anthropological research.[3]

The focus of the collections varied over time. Warner and Thomson made broadly comprehensive collections of Yolngu material culture, the Berndts and Mountford placed a stronger emphasis on Yolngu artworks and for Kupka, Groger-Wurm, and the Morphys, the main focus of collection was art. The change of emphasis reflects both the particular focus of the researchers and the changing nature of Yolngu society as it moved from a mobile hunter-gather base at the time of Warner's and Thomson's initial fieldwork to sedentarization on mission stations and government settlements.

The relationship between Yolngu and museums has been a dialogic process in which motivations, possibilities, and engagements have changed over time. However, partly because of the active involvement of Yolngu throughout, it is possible to see continuities in the developing trajectory rather than the discontinuities, which occurred elsewhere. In the century since the establishment of the first mission stations in their country, Yolngu, anthropologists, missionaries, curators, and collectors have been entangled in a value-creation process which has contributed to major changes in attitudes to Yolngu 'art'.[4] I have written about the history of Yolngu art in detail elsewhere (Morphy 2007), and here my focus is on the post-World War II era.

After the war, Methodist missions continued to market Aboriginal art, both as an economic resource and to present a positive view of Yolngu society to their congregations. The Reverend Edgar Wells, superintendent at Milingimbi from 1949 to 1959, opened up marketing opportunities for Yolngu paintings in the southern states and Europe and engaged with collectors and curators to encourage their recognition as fine art. Anthropologists Ronald and Catherine Berndt, A.P. Elkin, and Charles Mountford all became engaged with projects that would move Aboriginal art into the museums of fine art. The Berndts were concerned that Aboriginal art should be seen on its own terms, not positioned in relation to Western art history as 'primitive art' separated from the world of the present.[5] Aboriginal art was 'contemporary *not* primitive' and should be exhibited in art galleries just as the art produced by non-Indigenous Australians (Berndt and Berndt 1957). In the 1950s and 1960s, Ronald Berndt played a key role with others, in particular with Tony Tuckson of the Art Gallery of New South Wales, in shifting people's appreciation of Aboriginal art (Morphy 2007).

A crucial step in the process of recognizing Aboriginal art as contemporary Australian art was the intervention made by Stuart Scougall, an orthopaedic surgeon and collector of Aboriginal art, and Tony Tuckson. Tuckson had been greatly struck by bark paintings collected by Berndt that were exhibited at David Jones's commercial art gallery in Sydney in 1948. In 1958 and 1959, he took the opportunity of Scougall's sponsorship to accompany him on expeditions to the Northern Territory, making major collections of ironwood *pukumani* memorial poles from the Tiwi Islands and bark paintings from Yirrkala. The works were exhibited in the foyer of the Art Gallery of New South Wales the following year. Their inclusion was challenging to many, but over time, they have become an increasingly central part of the gallery's identity. In the years that followed, Aboriginal art became a major component of the Australian art world. All state cultural institutions have developed collections of Aboriginal art, and it has been acquired by leading international museums, such as the Metropolitan Museum of Art in New York and the Quai Branly in Paris.

Aboriginal art has provided a broad challenge to existing categorization of art in Australia as people have changed their understanding of Indigenous cultural production. Museum collections made by anthropologists have themselves changed categories as they entered different regimes of value. The Berndts, for example, used crayon drawings as a part of their field methodology, eliciting information by encouraging people to illustrate particular topics, from daily life to spirit conception. Yolngu responded with such enthusiasm and skill to this introduced method that the drawings were later the subject of a major exhibition at the AGNSW and have been included in UNESCO's Memory of the World Register. This symbolizes in some respects the productive relationships that developed between Yolngu and anthropologists in the development of museum collections, which opened possibilities for both.

Yolngu used their engagement with outsiders to learn about the power structures, systems of government, and values of European Australian society. Reflecting on his visit to the British Museum where a smaller installation of his work had been associated with *Enduring Civilisation*, the Yolngu artist Wukun Wanambi wrote,

> I feel *manymak* (good) sharing *Yolŋu madayin* (sacred Law) into English culture. England has sacred objects from other cultures. I want England to understand that we have a Law. I am happy to show our work because we are promoting Yolŋu culture into other worlds.[6]

In addition to making paintings for sale, art entered into syncretic dialogue with the Methodist missionaries. The most renowned case of this was the painting in 1962 of the Yirrkala Church Panels (Morphy 2007: 63). The Reverend Edgar Wells had moved to Yirrkala and was approached by Narritjin Maymuru to include Yolngu sacred art in the new church he was constructing. Two 3-metre-high Masonite panels were painted with designs reflecting the spiritual ties that Yolngu have to their land. The panels were installed on either side of the altar of the newly built Yirrkala church. In placing the panels, the Yolngu were making a strong statement about the equivalence in value of their religious practices and Christianity.

However, Yolngu had another reason for placing their paintings in the church: their concern over recent encroachments on their land by mining companies. Yolngu saw the paintings as evidencing their title to the land. In the following year, 1963, they sent typewritten petitions to the Commonwealth Parliament stuck on sheets of bark with borders painted with sacred designs. While the Bark Petitions did not immediately result in the recognition of their rights, their impact was considerable and set in train a process that eventually resulted in the recognition of their title to their land through the passing of the Aboriginal Land Rights Act (Northern Territory), 1976.

The Yolngu were fortunate in that they were able to continue to live and make adjustments to their new way of life with relatively little interference from the outside. They continued to produce 'art' on a regular basis for ceremonial performances, and, perhaps most importantly, they never lost effective control of most of their traditional lands. The processes of value creation they engaged in with other Australians over time had positive outcomes in that their art objects became both evidence in court cases and objects of desire. The works gained new value just as they became objects distributed through a wider domain. In a sense, the Yolngu had sent their material culture objects out as emissaries, and the initial return had been the wider recognition of the power of their cultural production, which simultaneously became a medium for the expression of their rights. The fact that the Yirrkala Bark Petition occupies a place in Parliament House in Canberra next a copy of the Magna Carta signals the extent to which Yolngu have produced material objects which have a powerful place in the national imagination.

Yolngu agency in the building of collections

In 2004, Frances Morphy and I were researching the Blue Mud Bay native title claim. The court case required the applicants to establish continuity of attachment to place over time, to demonstrate that they had customary ways of establishing rights in land, and to provide a comprehensive cultural mapping of the region under claim (Morphy and Morphy 2006). As part of our research, we brought with us documentary material from museum collections that might be useful in the court case, in particular from the Thomson and Berndt collections, which were made during the initial years of Australian government control of the region. One of the resources that we brought with us was a map of the region produced in 1946 for Ronald Berndt by Yolngu people, including Narritjin Maymuru and his brother Nänyin. The maps provided detailed coverage of the place names across the region, including details of their meaning and the clan affiliations. One day, we were looking at the maps laid out on a dune overlooking a stretch of Blue Mud Bay. Dhukal Wirrpanda, Narritjin's son in law, after taking in some of the details that were recorded, sat back and reflected on the vision of the old people in making the maps, knowing that they would be useful in the future. 'How clever of those old people', he said. In the end, we did not have to use the Berndt maps since Yolngu knowledge of the country remained impressive. However, Dhukal's comments open up the question of the extent to which Yolngu participation in anthropological research and in the building of ethnographic collections was as much directed to future Yolngu as it was to the non-Yolngu world. To what extent were Narritjin and Nänyin looking forward in time? Again, in this case, there may be more of a coincidence between Yolngu motivations and the motivations of the researchers than people have previously allowed.

The relationships that developed between Yolngu and outsiders were often close, and material culture objects were part of that process of exchange. The conversations were 'both ways' as Yolngu would say. Thomson records in his notebook having conversations with Yolngu at a goose-hunters camp in the Arafura swamp, elaborating on the principles of Linnaean taxonomy to demonstrate that Europeans, like Yolngu, have complex ways of classifying the natural world. Certainly, by the 1950s, Yolngu were well aware of the presence of collections in museums in the southern states of Australia and began to visit them. Kupka, working at Milingimbi, recorded how the clan leader Djawa had earlier sent collections from a mortuary ritual for his father to a museum in Sydney so that they could be preserved longer. Jessica de Largy Healy, a French anthropologist who undertook research at Milingimbi 40 years after Kupka's research, describes how warmly he was remembered and was told details of the ways in which he was taught by the painters and incorporated through classificatory kinship within the community. De Largy Healy in turn became kin with Kupka across the generations through her incorporation within the same kin system.[7]

Some of the best evidence that Yolngu explicitly saw the recording of their culture by outsiders as being of benefit to succeeding generations of Yolngu comes not from the material culture collections but from films. Yolngu have participated in documentary filmmaking since the early days of colonization. A number of films of Yolngu life, including ritual performances, were made in the 1940s. In 1971, when Ian Dunlop began working on what subsequently became the Yirrkala Film Project, Yolngu were able to exercise considerable agency over the way the filming developed (see Deveson 2011). On many occasions, Yolngu prefaced filming sessions by contextualizing the film in relation to its future use. The films, they stated, were being made for future generations to show them what life was like and to record ceremonies and songs so that subsequent generations could learn from them. That view of their purpose fundamentally influenced what was filmed. Working to the west of the Yolngu region a few years later, the anthropologist Les Hiatt and the filmmaker Kim McKenzie got a similar response when recording an Anbara hollow log coffin ceremony (McKenzie 1980).

It is impossible to know when Yolngu first became aware of the potential of film for the process of knowledge transmission, but my belief is this awareness arose at the very beginning of familiarity with the process. Yolngu see different means of passing on knowledge as complementary and apply the same word, *djorra* (document), to their own cultural productions and to introduced media, from writing to film.[8] In discussing the complementary role of bark paintings and introduced media while planning an exhibition at the Kluge Ruhe centre for Aboriginal Art at the University of Virginia, the Yolngu filmmaker Ishmael Marika commented in 2018 that 'bark painting as documentation came before new media'.[9] Yolngu remember events from the past that were filmed and at which people took photographs. Soon after we began working with Yolngu, people made occasional requests to access particular recordings we had made. They have always been aware of the museum collections that have been made and have again on occasions accessed them. The practice of anthropologists, from Ronald and Catherine Berndt onwards, in maintaining communication with Yolngu reinforced the idea that the increasingly distributed archive of Yolngu material culture was potentially accessible to the Yolngu.

However, until the turn of the twenty-first century, access was difficult. The majority of collecting institutions were in south-east Australia, image production was costly, and travel was very expensive. Nonetheless, some Yolngu did visit cultural institutions, often in association with cultural performances or political events. In recent years, access has become much easier, both because of increased opportunities to visit collections and as a consequence of the digital revolution, which has meant that communities in more remote regions can access digitized copies of material held in cultural institutions. Yirrkala itself has set up the Mulka Knowledge Centre as a facility for the digital repatriation of images as well as a local archive and museum. Today, the Mulka Centre plays the role that outside filmmakers did in the past, recording cultural events for the Yolngu and disseminating them to the world outside. In many cases today, the recorders are the Yolngu themselves.

Developments over the 80 years that have elapsed since the establishment of the mission station at Yirrkala can be viewed as a process of exchange in which Yolngu have ultimately gained a degree of control over the dispersed archive of their material culture through the very success of releasing it in the first place. The value-creation process that began with that original release has resulted in widespread recognition of their cultural forms and has increased the opportunities for them to reconnect with their dispersed collections. In recent years, funding has increasingly been made available for Indigenous access to collections both remotely through digital repatriation and through the involvement of community members in research and exhibition development. Many projects have been initiated by community members (West 2008); others have been generated from the museums.

Reflecting back

In detailing the Yolngu case, I have illustrated a developing trajectory in which Yolngu agency was integral to the process of building collections. I have argued that the making of collections was part of a value-creation process and exchange of knowledge that mediated relationships between Yolngu and the colonists over the period of time that has elapsed since European colonization. In the 1920s, in the final stages of Australia's colonization, the invasion of Aboriginal land was still ongoing. Over a period of 80 years, the Yolngu have moved from the frontier of European colonization, potentially subject to punitive expeditions, to becoming incorporated within the nation-state. Over time, the Yolngu played a significant role in the wider struggle that saw Aboriginal people in the Northern Territory achieve land rights. The anthropologists, missionaries, government officials, and others who entered into exchanges were integral to the process of value creation and were in many cases co-agents in a process of persuasion.

During that time, the focus of anthropological research has changed, not only as a result of processes internal to the discipline but also because Yolngu society is itself in a process of change. The anthropologists who built the collections were both in their time and ahead of their time. They did engage with Australian policy, many as critics and some such as A.P. Elkin as advocates for the better implementation of government policy. In the 1920s, few Australians could have even conceived of Aboriginal land rights legislation. The invasion of Aboriginal land was still underway. Aboriginal art was largely unrecognized, none was included in the collections of the state galleries of fine art. When the anthropologist Bill Stanner coined the phrase 'the great Australian silence' in his Boyer Lectures of 1968, he was referring not only to the silence about Australia's colonial past but also about the failure to include and acknowledge Indigenous Australians in the present.[10]

I now examine the extent to which we can see similar kinds of collaborative relationships – with agency on both sides – in the nineteenth and early twentieth centuries. In the first two cases of Tasmania and the Kwatkwat artist Tommy McRae, the surviving collections are meagre and the colonial context overwhelming – the preamble to 'the great Australian silence'. Until recently, the received history of anthropology emphasized a paradigm break between the era of museum anthropology associated with evolutionary theory and the cultural relativism that became a dominant trope in the twentieth century. Such a perspective is in harmony with the critique of the discipline that sees anthropology as developing in tandem with the colonial enterprise, providing ideological support and facilitating its objectives.

My own analysis reaches different conclusions by seeing anthropology as an integral part of a process of change in attitudes to and conception of colonized people. What the received histories mask is the agency of the Indigenous people involved in building the collections and the fact that the researchers and collectors themselves influenced the attitudinal changes that occurred. Rather than emphasizing discontinuity between the anthropology of the nineteenth and early twentieth centuries and the present day, it is important to see the underlying continuities: the similar relationships at play and the overarching motivation to understand and interpret cultural difference. The failure to acknowledge the importance of museum collections to anthropology's subsequent history and its engagement with Indigenous societies both distorts the historical process and creates barriers to the development of positive relationships between today's Indigenous communities and the museums that house their collections. In the concluding sections of this chapter, I reflect back on the earlier history in the light of these observations.

Engaging with strangers and with invaders

Indigenous Australians manage their land on the basis of kinship, religion, and a deep knowledge of the environment. Many of the accounts of the engagement of Indigenous Australians with Europeans who crossed or entered their country are of initial cautious welcome. Sometimes this took the form of rituals of welcome, which were at the same time demonstrations of power: a number of men moving forward in unison, arms raised, spears in hand, finally thrusting the spears into the ground in front of the visitors. Such a performance almost certainly met Cook's crew when they landed at Botany Bay in the south of the continent on 29 April 1770, and a similar performance took place in the north on 22 January 1803 when members of Matthew Flinders's crew landed on Morgan Island in Blue Mud Bay. Indigenous Australians were welcoming the visitors and introducing them to their country. And on some occasions, this resulted in friendly relations being established in the short term.

That was not always the case. In retrospect, those interactions have to be seen as a prelude to invasion and colonization even when that was not the intention at the time. At Botany Bay and Morgan Island, both meetings were first encounters with Europeans. Both encounters led to shots being fired at the Aboriginal people, and on Morgan Island at least one Yolngu person was killed. From the time of the First Fleet in 1788, whatever those rituals of diplomacy and acts of generosity meant to Indigenous Australians, they were not going to prevent their land from being taken away and the loss of freedom that this entailed.

The colonization of Tasmania and south-east Australia resulted in the decimation of the Aboriginal population as a result of disease, the destruction of their way of life, and, in many, cases massacres. The speed at which these events occurred was devastating. Aboriginal people took advantage of the few opportunities that they had to engage in the economy that was replacing them in their country. They had to work on the sheep and cattle stations, to become dependent on the generosity of the invaders. As the colony expanded, their rights diminished; the space they were allowed to occupy was routinely reduced, and their rights were perpetually being lost.

In the spaces allowed, they continued to create a life for themselves. One of the ways in which they engaged with the colonists was by continuing a trade in material culture objects, weapons and fibre arts, ceremonial attire and decorative objects. Many fine objects were made at mission stations and government settlements and sold in the local market. When museums were established in the separate colonies, many of these objects ended up as part of their collections, and others were traded and exchanged overseas. The majority of carved wooden objects, the beautifully engraved shields, clubs, and boomerangs now in museum collections were made by now anonymous craftsmen at mission stations and government settlements.

There was a market for Aboriginal products, and implicitly, the purchasers were recognizing the aesthetic values and skills involved in their production. Many of those who made collections early on were indeed among the colonists who were most sympathetic to Indigenous concerns. Far more of the objects that have ended up in museum collections came from this origin then came from the field of battle. But they can, nonetheless, understandably, be seen as the products of servitude and effective imprisonment.

Tasmania

Tasmanian Aboriginal people, the subject of some of the earliest ethnographic descriptions, were the victims of a genocidal colonial process in which they were removed wholesale from their land. The survivors were forcibly removed to an offshore island and effectively spent the rest of their lives in different forms of custody. Most of the early collections of Tasmanian material culture were taken to European museums. The British Museum holds the only surviving kelp basket from the nineteenth century, which was sent to the Great Exhibition of 1851 – an exquisite and delicate object that was selected to illustrate the potential of kelp as a raw material. For over a century, the descendants of those few who survived the killings were largely denied even an identity. The fact that many descendants of Tasmanian Aboriginal people continued to live on the islands of Bass Strait, some families on mainland Tasmania and elsewhere, was almost erased from history: Aboriginal Tasmanians were declared by Europeans to be 'extinct'. The gap between the first encounters of Europeans with Tasmanian Aboriginal people and the decimation of their population was short. Engagement moved quickly from the curiosity of the Enlightenment to the genocide of the colonial encounter.

Two of the most important surviving collections from Tasmania were made by people who played significant roles in the cultural life of the British colony of Tasmania – Joseph Milligan and Lady Jane Franklin. Joseph Milligan was a Scottish surgeon who arrived in Hobart in 1830, towards the end of what has been referred to as the Black War – the final stage of the genocide of the Tasmanian Aboriginal people. In 1835, the majority of the surviving Aboriginal population, some 300 people, were removed to Wybalena on Flinders Island in the Bass Strait. In December 1843, Milligan was appointed 'superintendent of and medical officer for the Aboriginals'. In 1846, he supervised the return of the 46 people who had survived to be resettled at Oyster Cove. Milligan was the secretary of the Royal Society of Tasmania from 1848 until 1860. He advocated for improved conditions for the people in Oyster Cove and was interested in Aboriginal culture and language. He made some of the most detailed vocabularies of Tasmanian dialects and made collections of material culture objects for the embryonic Tasmanian Museum. Objects collected by him are in the collections of the Australian Museum in Sydney, and on his return to London, he coordinated the display at the 1851 Great Exhibition as commissioner for Tasmania. Milligan included shell necklaces, the kelp water container, and a model canoe. After the 1851 exhibition closed, Milligan gave the Tasmanian artefacts to the British Museum.

An important Tasmanian Aboriginal collection at the Pitt Rivers Museum was originally collected by Lady Jane Franklin, the wife of Sir John Franklin, governor of Tasmania from 1836 to 1843. She took the first steps in establishing Tasmania's cultural institutions, including the society which in 1848 became the first Royal Society outside the United Kingdom. She was sympathetic to the plight of Aboriginal people on Flinders Island and decided to adopt an Aboriginal girl, Mathinna, in order to show how it was possible to civilize people by bringing them up in the right environment. However, when the Franklins were recalled from Tasmania, Mathinna was returned to Flinders Island and, finally, to Oyster Cove, near where she died in c. 1852.

It is no wonder that today's descendants of the local source community have had to participate in a brave, at times contentious and complex, process of reengagement with collections from their past. Establishing their agency over collections and asserting their continuing historical presence has been a fundamental part of the process. Tasmanian Aboriginal people play an increasingly significant role in the curation of collections and have engaged with the past and with their heritage in museum collections through the medium of art. Julie Gough's artwork *The Lost World (Part2)*, 2013, exhibited simultaneously at the Cambridge Museum of Archaeology and Anthropology and Contemporary Art Tasmania, Hobart, involves the virtual repatriation of Tasmanian stone tools from the Cambridge collection by placing photographs of the objects back in the place of collection. Kelp baskets and water carriers are now being made again by artists such as Verna Nichols, and Lola Greeno has gained renown for her exquisite shell necklaces.

The recognition of Tommy McRae

Tommy McRae Yakaduna of the Kwatkwat people was born in the 1830s, around the time of the establishment in 1834 of Portland, the first British settlement in what later became the state of Victoria. Much of Victoria provided excellent grazing land, and Aboriginal land was quickly expropriated. McRae's country was in the north of the state on the Victorian/New South Wales border. The Aboriginal population had been greatly reduced even before the Ovens River goldrush brought an influx of 26,000 miners into his country in the 1850s.[11]

The relatively few records of McRae's life show him to have been a remarkable person. He worked as a stockman on a number of properties, sold fish to the settlers, raised poultry, made artefacts for sale, and raised a large family. For much of his life, he lived at Lake Moodemere near Wahgunyah on the Murray River. Aboriginal people came increasingly under the control of the state, with government policy directed to moving them off their land and into reserves. Cooper and Urry (1981) show how McRae himself resisted the move to state institutions and maintained his relatively autonomous life, occupying the niches that were allowed him. But in 1892, new regulations were introduced to allow the Board for the Protection of the Aborigines to commit children to institutions without their parents' consent. For a decade, McRae struggled to keep his large family together, moving backwards and forwards across the Victorian and New South Wales borders. But by 1897, all of his children had been seized from him (Cooper and Urry 1981: 83).

None of the artefacts or possum-fur cloaks that he made for sale can today be attributed to him. Possum-fur cloaks – spectacular and impressive garments – were made for sale, but none of the early cloaks are known by the maker's name. Today, shields from south-east Australia are recognized for their fine craftsmanship and powerful geometric designs. Researchers are beginning to try to identify the styles of individual craftspeople and the locations in which they worked (Jones 2015: 78). Some artefacts made by McRae may be in museum collections, but as yet, none have been identified.

Tommy McRae also produced a large number of drawings, and these have gained increasing renown. He began making drawings as early as the 1860s, and the earliest ones went under the name of Tommy Barnes. His drawings subsequently impressed Roderick Kilborn, the telegraph master at Wahgunyah and subsequently a wine maker. Kilborn in effect acted as his agent, commissioning drawings to be gifted to a departing governor of Victoria and on another occasion arranging for two notebooks to be sent to Andrew Lang in London. The drawings were done in ink on sheets of paper or in small sketch books. McRae's style was unique, producing exquisite drawings evoking Aboriginal life, many of them portraying sets of dancers, depicting their body paintings and ceremonial attire in fine detail. He also documented the changes that were going on around him – a ship in sail, the European pastoralists at ease, the escaped convict Buckley, and Chinese miners on the Goldfields (Cooper and Urry 1981; Sayers 1994; von Zinnenburg Carroll 2014). But on the whole, it seems that his market required images depicting Aboriginal life as it was. Some 400 are known to have survived, fragile works on paper valued by the people who kept them. As works of art, they were of ambiguous status. As figurative drawings in ink on paper, they were viewed neither as Aboriginal art nor as European art. Their anomalous status is captured in the almost contradictory words of the distinguished Australian art historian and curator Daniel Thomas who, on the same page, described McCrae's works as among 'the first masterpieces of cross-cultural art' (2011: 3) and later as 'lowly tourist-trade and local-souvenir art [which] nevertheless has extraordinary aesthetic force' (ibid: 4).[12]

Thomas was writing at the time of McRae's belated recognition as an important colonial artist. His drawings were quite widely known at the turn of the twentieth century. A number had been reproduced in publications in his lifetime and many more in the following years. On many occasions early on, they were reproduced as unattributed works of an anonymous native, even though his name was clearly known by many of those who published them. Andrew Lang, who wrote the preface to Langlogh Parker's books *Australian Legendary Tales*, used McRae's drawings as illustrations. They were attributed to 'an Aborigine'. Subsequent editions have remedied the omission of his name. McRae's drawings were also included in a number of exhibitions of Aboriginal art. In the 1929 *Aboriginal Art* exhibition in Melbourne, they were first exhibited under the name of the artist, but when they were sent to America for the 1942 touring exhibition *Art of Australia*, which opened at the Metropolitan Museum of Art in New York, they again became anonymous. It was not until the end of the twentieth century, when Aboriginal art from north and central Australia began to share the gallery spaces with non-Indigenous art, that McRae gained widespread recognition for his work (Sayers 1994).

McRae's drawings were appreciated in his lifetime and were arguably a commercial success. The relationships he established meant that in his battles with authorities, he was supported by Kilborn and others who admired his drawings and advocated on his behalf.[13] But on balance, his story is of someone whose people's land was taken away from them by invaders, whose children were taken away because of his race, and whose name was taken away from his artworks on many of the occasions they were used in publications or hung in exhibitions.

This explains in part the positive response of descendants of the artists to Andrew Sayers book, *Aboriginal Artists of the Nineteenth Century*. The book, which included an important chapter from Carol Cooper, focussed on the work of three main artists – Tommy McRae; William Barak (1824–1903) from the 'Yarrayarra' (Wurundjeri) tribe, also of Victoria; and Mickey of Ulladulla in New South Wales (1820–1891). In a symposium at the National Museum of Australia to celebrate the twentieth anniversary of the book, one of Barak's descendants, Joy Murphy Wandin, stated that the book was transformative, providing 'another window to explore exactly where I've come from' (Bonyhady and Hinkson 2015). Jonathon Jones recalled that, when he first encountered *Aboriginal Artists* as a university undergraduate,

> It felt like the first time that Koori art history, the history of my people, had actually been acknowledged and the important work of my ancestors had been so recognized. It was the first time I could see myself within a book and see where I'd come from.
>
> (Ibid 2015)

The history of Tommy McRae's art and its misrecognition and lack of recognition has stimulated works by contemporary Indigenous artists such as Vernon Ah Kee. Ah Kee generalizes the reception of Aboriginal art across time through relating descriptions of McRae's art to his own body (von Zinnenburg Carroll 2014: 22).[14]

Tommy McRae had limited recognition in his lifetime, and until recently, few of his works ended up in institutional collections. However, those who recognized the value in his fragile works and acquired them, and whose descendants ensured their survival for over a century, played a major role in making Tommy McRae part of Australia's art history. The survival of his works becomes a means to reassign the past to the present and create continuity and renewal. Just as in Tasmania, it has opened up multiple modes of engagement with collections and archives, with historical documents and anthropological writings. Possum-skin cloaks are being remade, genealogies and documents become resources to be explored and repositioned, and aesthetic practice becomes a strong means of exploring and asserting identity.

Spencer and the recognition of Aboriginal art

At the end of the nineteenth century, Baldwin Spencer and Francis Gillen played key roles in the development of a fieldwork-based anthropology.[15] Spencer and Gillen's writings had an immediate impact in Europe in providing basic ethnography for books by Fraser, Freud, and Durkheim. Their ethnographic collections initially had a more limited impact. Indeed, in 1902, Spencer wrote, 'The ordinary public does not appreciate our collection but in the years to come it is some satisfaction to feel the ethnologists will do' (Mulvaney 2008). However, over time, their ethnographic collections have played a significant role in the value-creation processes that have resulted in the recognition of Aboriginal art.

The quality of their ethnographic collections, their resource as an archive for 'Aboriginal art', is not a result of happenstance but reflects their very deep appreciation of, and knowledge about, Aboriginal society. Their collections were exceptionally well documented through the photographs they took in the field, their publications, their field notebooks, and entries in museum catalogues. The richness of their ethnographic data and analysis was integral to fostering broader attitudinal changes towards Aboriginal culture and society. In both cases – recognizing Indigenous aesthetic accomplishments and recognizing and valuing Aboriginal society in its own terms – there was a considerable time lag between collecting and researching and the positive outcomes.[16] Perhaps because of this, the important role that Spencer and Gillen's work and collections have played in Australian art history is often uncomfortably acknowledged and recognized (see Stephen 2017).

Tony Bennett (2018: 22) insightfully characterizes Spencer as 'a Mancunian liberal schooled in the traditions of John Stuart Mill, struggling to reconcile those traditions with the realities of the frontier that supported his practice'. He goes on to note that Spencer and Gillen's fieldwork depended on 'the relative shift from the killings of the frontier wars to the more regularized forms of biopolitical governance that characterized the post-Federation establishment of the state-regulated "Aboriginal domain"'.

While there is unquestionably truth in that analysis, it underestimates the active role that Spencer and Gillen played in challenging the ways in which the colonizers treated Aboriginal people and the attitudes they had toward them. The response of a police constable M.C. Cowle to the publication of their first book, *The Native Tribes of Central Australia*, reflected the attitudes of many when he accused them of creating 'a cult of Spencer and Gillenism that showed the Aborigines as human beings' (cited in Morphy 2012: 550). Earlier as a police magistrate in 1891, Gillen had taken the almost unprecedented action in charging a police officer, MC Wilshire, with the murder of Aboriginal people during a policing operation (Mulvaney and Calaby 1985: 125). He was subsequently acquitted.

I have written extensively on Spencer and Gillen's place in the history of anthropology and argued that they played a key role in the process of transformation which led to a recognizably modern anthropology. My focus here is on the role that Spencer, in particular, played in the process of gaining recognition for Aboriginal art. Spencer and Gillen's influence can be seen operating in three separate ways – through their writings, in the role Spencer played in the developing Australian art world, and through the resource of the material collections.

At the end of the nineteenth century, Australian Aboriginal art was largely unrecognized. It was not included in the collections of art museums and was largely absent from writings about art. This situation continued throughout the first two thirds of the twentieth century and is still not entirely resolved. It was not so much that Aboriginal art was excluded – it was just not seen as the same category of thing as European art. The reasons for this are highly complex and connected both to the formal properties of Aboriginal art and to the positioning of Aboriginal society in an evolutionary past. The category of fine art that developed in the eighteenth and nineteenth centuries was primarily centred on Europe's present art practice and its presumed historical antecedents.

Spencer and Gillen's early writings on central Australian art engaged with European art discourse on the history of design and the relationship between technique and form. They drew attention to the aesthetic aspects of material objects and the technical skills involved in their production. Their books were richly illustrated. But the primary focus of their writings was on the cultural contexts of the work. They provided insights that have subsequently proved central to understanding the religious significance of many forms of Aboriginal art.

It was much later on, when undertaking research at Oenpelli in Arnhem Land that he understood for the first time that Aboriginal art, though different from European art, involved a similar skill set and aesthetic sensibility. Oenpelli is set beside a waterhole on the edge of the Arnhem Land escarpment. It is a place of incredible beauty. The steep slopes of the scarp are fractured and cut through with crevices so that it is possible to walk into the rock face and clamber up it, rest on rock platforms, and shelter from the heat of the day beneath the overhangs. The walls and ceilings of the rock shelters are covered with paintings, often superimposed on top of one another, representing the work of many generations of artists. The most recent style is characterized by X-ray figures of animals and images of supernatural beings and spirit figures. The wet season huts where people camped beside the lagoon were covered with similar paintings. Spencer writes almost lyrically about watching an artist as he painted:

> Today I found a native who, apparently, had nothing better to do than to sit quietly in the camp evidently enjoying himself . . . he held [his brush] like a civilized artist . . . he did the line work, often very fine

> and regular, with much the same freedom and precision as a Japanese or Chinese artist doing his most beautiful wash-work with his brush.
> (Spencer 1928: 792–793)

Spencer found that there was as much difference between the artists' work as would be the case with English artists and found it affirming that their qualitative judgements coincided with his own. The analogies Spencer draws here are highly salient. He saw, in the work of the artists, characteristics that he associated with 'civilized' art. The artists painted for pleasure, were highly skilled and aesthetically sensitive, and exercised freedom within a tradition of technical accomplishment (see Morphy 2013).

Spencer's growing recognition of shared characteristics that connected Aboriginal art to other art traditions can be connected to the role he played in the colonial art world of Melbourne and his relationships with artists, curators, and arts administrators. Spencer was a major figure in the institutional development of Australian art in the late nineteenth and early twentieth centuries, both through his lobbying of government and his sponsorship of artists. In Melbourne, he was a member of the Society of Artists and lectured and gave presentations on Aboriginal art, and, indeed, his initial exhibition of western Arnhem Land bark paintings was in the Society's gallery.

He worked closely with Sydney Ure Smith to influence government policy and in publishing and promoting work by Australian artists. Ure Smith's journal, *Art and Australia*, from the 1920s on began to include a series of articles on Aboriginal art in particular by the Australian modernist Margaret Preston. Preston followed Spencer in visiting Oenpelli to look at the rock art that he had made people aware of through his writings and lectures. She established close friendships with anthropologists and spent considerable time researching museum collections. In 1941, Daryl Lindsay became an innovative director of the National Gallery of Victoria, and it was under Lindsay that Aboriginal art was exhibited for the first time in the National Gallery of Victoria in 1943 under the umbrella of *Primitive Art*. The exhibition was curated by the German anthropologist and jurist Leonard Adam. Many of the works included in the exhibition were ones that Spencer and Gillen had collected and donated to the Melbourne Museum.

In the first half of the twentieth century, Spencer and Gillen's collections and the images reproduced in their publication began to influence Australian art practice. Anne Stephen shows how the avant-garde artist and filmmaker Len Lye had used Baldwin Spencer's recordings of the central Australian designs as the inspiration for his film *Tusalava* (Stephen 2017). Spencer and Gillen's wax cylinder recordings of central Australian songs had a major impact on Percy Grainger, who described them as 'lithe and graceful as snakes and highly complex in their rhythmic irregularities . . . too complex for untrained modern ears'. Their published images began to influence Australian art and design from the paintings and prints of Margaret Preston to the work of designers, such Gert Sellheim and Nancy Mackenzie.

The recognition of Aboriginal art on its own terms but coeval with other world art traditions was a long and complex process that involved change in the Western category of fine art (Morphy 2007). The process was in harmony with changes that occurred in the recognition of non-Western art more generally that happened over a century, stretching from the end of the nineteenth to the latter half of the twentieth century. In many respects, it is still a process underway. A sign of these changes, though not the cause of them as is sometimes assumed, has been the movement of non-Western art, which was previously positioned outside the Western canon of fine art, onto the walls, and into the collections of museums of fine art. However, it was the collections of ethnographic museums, which had acknowledged the value of the works as aesthetic forms quite independently of the Western fine art category, that provided the resource for the art museums when they finally admitted non-Western art. The history of Spencer and Gillen's collections in Australia provide a prime example of this process.

Bark paintings collected by Spencer in 1912 were a feature of the first major exhibition of Australian Aboriginal Art in 1929 at the National Museum of Victoria and were the main Aboriginal works exhibited in the 1941 *Art of Australia* exhibition at the Metropolitan Museum of Art in New York, which subsequently toured America. They were exhibited in Melbourne in the 1943 *Primitive Art* exhibition and travelled overseas to critical acclaim in the 1993 *Aratjara* exhibition at London's Hayward Gallery.

It is no accident that Spencer and Gillen's collections have made a significant contribution to the process of value creation associated with Aboriginal art and have played a role in challenging the evolutionary hierarchy that placed Aboriginal society on the lower rungs of the ladder of human evolution. Spencer challenged those ideas both in his writings and through the quality of the collections. Spencer and Gillen were able to build their collections and add to their value through documentation because of the generally positive relationships they had with the people with whom they worked. In the context of their times, both were motivated to create a better environment for Aboriginal people but viewed the future for Aboriginal people pessimistically and saw their eventual assimilation as inevitable (Morphy 2012).

We have no detailed accounts of the motivation of the Arrernte people who cooperated in building the collections that Spencer and Gillen made. We have plenty of indirect information that Aboriginal people engaged strongly in the collecting process – people knew of their impending arrival and gathered to sell artefacts. Spencer and Gillen facilitated ceremonial performances at a time when it was increasingly difficult for Aboriginal people to get the resources and commandeer the space. Gillen's diaries and letters show the warmth of his relationship with Arrernte people. In the context of the times, Spencer and Gillen's relationship with Arrernte people was close. Joel Liddle Perrurle, a descendant of Irrapmwe Peltharre, an Arrernte leader they worked closely with writes, 'What is pretty clear though is that both men had developed meaningful relationships and trust with their informants' (Batty, forthcoming). While acknowledging that Spencer and Gillen used language that is quite unacceptable today, Liddle Perrurle writes, 'It's clear that Gillen and (Peltharre) were friends and worked well together' (Batty, forthcoming).

The photographs, films, and wax recordings that formed the basis of Spencer's persuasive lectures to Melbourne society were also screened by Gillen to the Arrernte people in the courtyard of the Telegraph Station in Alice Springs. Spencer and Gillen's writings and photographs have been an ever-present reminder of the presence of Arrernte people in the town. The Indigenous naming of the landscape recorded in their writings has been mapped into the township of Alice Springs and the surrounding region partly as a result of their publications. On Spencer's recommendation, reserves were established in the Northern Territory that 60 years on with the passing of the Northern Territory land Rights Act became the first areas of land transferred to Aboriginal ownership. One of those first established was indeed Hermannsburg today renamed Ntaria. And today, many of the sites in the region mentioned in their publications have become protected sacred sites of heritage places.

Spencer and Gillen's collections have been made available online in a project linking the museums that house them with the local communities (Gibson et al. 2019). As in the Yolngu case, the richness of the material enables members of source communities to see Indigenous agency at the heart of the process. Reflecting on their publications, Liddle Perrurle writes,

> I've had to 'sift' through [their writings] while keeping in mind that it's not necessarily Spencer and Gillen teaching me, they were merely the conveyors of messages. It's the Akngerrepate's (Elders) that offer this knowledge and therefore, I feel a sense of responsibility to treat the work with great care, admiration and respect. It's also our responsibility as Arrernte people to learn from their works and integrate the knowledges into our lives.

As Batty (2018: 58) writes, 'The descendants of the Aboriginal groups Spencer and Gillen documented are perhaps the most avid excavators of their ethnography'.

Conclusion

The collections reviewed in this chapter are very different in character. They can be seen as part of an overlapping colonial trajectory that has resulted in the incorporation of Indigenous Australians within an externally imposed nation-state. The state of Victoria was colonized initially from Tasmania. In Tommy McRae's lifetime, the Aboriginal people of Victoria suffered a catastrophic encounter similar to that endured by the Tasmanians. Baldwin Spencer arrived in Melbourne towards the end of McRae's life and would have been well aware of the appalling recent history. The end of the nineteenth century did not see the end of the invasion of Aboriginal land – the final massacres were yet to come, and children continued to be taken from their parents – but we begin to enter a time in which in some parts of Australia, the invasion was to take a different course.

The collections belong to very different colonial space-time zones. This has had a consequence for how the descendants of the producers view them and is also reflected in the nature and quality of the collections. The Tasmanian collections were made by survivors of a process of colonization during which they were literally hunted in a military operation. McRae's drawings were done at a later stage, when the gold rush and pastoralism had driven Aboriginal people off their land. They were made at a time when government policy was to move people to reserves and government settlements and when children were being forcibly separated from their parents. The objects in museum collections are rare survivors from a time when Aboriginal people were being obliterated from the imagination and concerns of the European population. Many objects were made for sale, but few ended up in museum collections.

Spencer and Gillen's collections overlapped with 'McRae's time' in Victoria but were made in a different colonial space-time. Gillen, as an operator of the Overland Telegraph, was there at the early stages of the colonization of central Australia, which, as in Victoria, was led by pastoralists. The environment was less favourable to pastoralism, and the European population of the Northern Territory remained a tiny minority. Missionaries were able to create a buffer between the Aboriginal population and the colonizers, and Aboriginal people became the main labour force on the cattle stations. It became possible for colonial officials like Gillen to play a more significant role in ameliorating colonial violence while, in Bennett's terms, introducing a 'state regulated domain'.

One sign of the difference is that the Arrernte population has increased since European colonization. Many continue to speak Arrernte, and they have retained ownership of much of their land, albeit through a process of continuous struggle. The collections made on their country were made at the beginning of the development of modern fieldwork-based anthropology. Spencer and Gillen's collections have survived almost in their entirety because they were destined from the beginning to reside in cultural institutions whose raison d'être is to enable their survival for future generations.

The Yolngu collections were made at a time when massacres were on the edge of becoming impossible, when Aboriginal people could have a sense that the collaborative relationships that they attempted to establish with outsiders would possibly succeed. The builders of collections were, on the whole, people who shared in the Yolngu agenda, and colonial time was beginning to change as the Indigenous struggle for rights began to have an impact on the urban settler society. A shared dialogue was developing which continues into the present. Not all collections were well documented, but the majority were. The primary destination of the Yolngu collections was, as with Spencer and Gillen's, the ethnography museum. However, in the second half of the twentieth century, as the value-creation process progressed, a much wider market developed as people began to collect Aboriginal art.

In each of these locations or regions, from Arnhem Land to Tasmania, the recognition of Indigenous rights has had a major impact over the past 50 years. However, past historical circumstances have resulted in very different outcomes. Land rights in most parts of southern Australia and Queensland are much harder to achieve than in parts of northern and central Australia. The resource of collections and the potential value they have to individuals and community varies enormously, according to factors such as scarcity, quality of documentation, colonial history, history of collection, and contemporary cultural production. In the case of Yolngu collections, people today are able to see a continuity that links them directly to their ancestors in an almost unbroken line to the beginning of colonization. The process is additive, and the Yolngu are both researchers on and contributors to the collections. In the case of Spencer and Gillen's collections, the discontinuity is greater, but the connections are still continuous, and the richness of the record brings the past to life. In the case of Tasmania and many areas of south-east Australia, the very scarcity of the material is a sign of past histories. The logic is that the material objects are going to be far more contested – yet, arguably, the value of their continuing survival is, if anything, greater. And the materiality of the collections transcends the breach of time.

People are conscious of gaps caused by the loss of language, separation from country, by the spread of pastoral properties, by mining, and, at times, by restrictions on movement. Population movement caused by changing government policy, from the breaking up of families to high levels of imprisonment, has had an effect on the transmission of knowledge and performance of ceremonies. Different lives have become associated with different bodies of knowledge, different musical genre, and different technical skills. While such changes in ways of life should not in themselves be seen as loss, the motivation for engagement for reconnecting with the past and for reclaiming technologies and meanings associated with places can be a very strong part of the present. Museum collections and archives provide a strong means of reengagement and of establishing agency in connecting with the past. And in a sense, that is precisely why the collections are there.

Notes

1 For details, see Nugent (2015: 163).

2 Warner's collection was distributed among many different institutions (Hamby 2008), and the main focus of his research was on religion and social organization. But the sense of his appreciation of Yolngu society is reflected in the title of his book *A Black Civilization.*

3 A number of very important collections were also made by missionaries who showed a strong interest in Yolngu material culture, including T.T. Webb, Edgar Wells, and Wilbur Chaseling.

4 While the relationships were at times antagonistic in retrospect, they can be seen to be broadly collaborative and in many respects Yolngu through their insistence on collaborative practice ensured that they were.

5 To the Berndts, '[Aboriginal art] is the external expression of the soul of a people . . . [the society] is concerned vitally with its own particular canons of beauty, having a social structure elastic enough to permit of individual treatment and variations on traditional themes, and the energy to have developed through the ages its own "school of art" '. (Berndt and Berndt 1950: 183).

6 The quotations from Wukun Wanambi are from the National Museum's entry on the exhibition. Consulted on 25 December 2018. www.nma.gov.au/exhibitions/unsettled/wukun_wanambi.

7 Milingimbi art was beginning to be widely marketed in the 1940s through the Methodist Overseas Mission and de Largy Healy shows how Kupka played a crucial mediating role between the two art worlds: the Yolngu and the European.

8 'Djorra' is a loanword from Makosarese acquired into Yolngu matha during the centuries when their shores were visited annually by Macassan trepangers. It is one of several hundred such loanwords.

9 Noted at a meeting on 16 November 2018.

10 In Stanner's memorable words, 'It is a structural matter, a view from a window which has been carefully placed to exclude a whole quadrant of the landscape. What may well have begun as a simple forgetting of other possible views turned under habit and over time into something like a cult of forgetfulness practised on a national scale' (Stanner 1969: 7).

11 Aboriginal people were barred from mining.

12 Von Zinnenburg Carroll (2014) writes insightfully about the contextual placing of Tommy McRae in Australian art history.

13 Von Zinnenburg Carroll (2014: 230), while acknowledging that in the end his ambitions were undermined by colonial government intervention, writes, 'He marks a moment of invention and change in the Aboriginal traditions of memorialization, and thereby presents new Indigenous strategies for cultural continuity'.

14 Ah Kee's 2007 self-portrait is captioned by the phrase *self-portrait (possesses some of the attributes of an artist)*, referencing how Tommy McRae was referred to by a reviewer.

15 Spencer's collaboration with Gillen began at the time of the Horn Expedition to central Australia in 1894 and continued until Gillen's death in 1912 (for details of their fieldwork, see Jones 2017; Batty 2018; Mulvaney and Calaby 1985). Spencer's main fieldwork in Arnhem Land and on the Tiwi Islands was undertaken in 1913.

16 Mulvaney summarizes their contribution as follows: 'Spencer's contribution 'was documenting 'Aboriginal artists at the moment of fatal impact . . . the first attempt at major documentation of art in its social context, using field notes, the camera and the systematic collection of material objects used in ceremonial activities. He rediscovered Arnhem Land bark painting and richly decorated Tiwi mortuary posts and organized the first documented collection of both art forms. He donated his entire collection to the nation' (Mulvaney and Calaby 1985: 359).

References

Batty, P. (2018) "Assembling the ethnographic field – the 1901–02 expedition of Baldwin Spencer and Francis Gillen," in Thomas, M. and Harris, A. (eds) *Expeditionary Anthropology – Teamwork, Travel and the 'Science of Man'*, pp. 37–63, Oxford: Berghahn.

Batty, P. (forthcoming) *Rites of Passage: The Expeditions of Spencer and Gillen*, Melbourne: Museum Victoria.

Bennett, T. (2018) "Museum transactions: negotiating knowledges, governing cultures," *Humanities Australia*, 9: 20–31.

Berndt, R.M. and Berndt, C.H. (1950) "Aboriginal art in central-western Northern Territory," *Meanjin*, 9 (3): 183–188.

Berndt, R.M. and Berndt, C.H. (1957) *The Art of Arnhem Land: An Exhibition of Australian Aboriginal Art. Arnhem Land Paintings on Bark and Carved Human Figures*, Perth: Art Gallery of Western Australia.

Bonyhady, T. and Hinkson, M. (2015) "The drawing master: Andrew Sayers' aboriginal artists of the nineteenth century," *Australian Book Review Arts*, 24 April, Friday.

Clendinnen, I. (2003) *Dancing with Strangers: Europeans and Australians at First Contact*, Cambridge: Cambridge University Press.

Coates, I. (2015) "Let us her no more of Pigeon," in Sculthorpe, G., Carty, J., Morphy, H., Nugent, M., Coates, I., Bolton, L. and Jones, J. (eds) *Indigenous Australia: Enduring Civilisation*, pp. 168–184, London: British Museum Press.

Cooper, C. and Urry, J. (1981) "Art, aborigines and Chinese – a nineteenth century drawing by the Kwatkwatartist Tommy McRae," *Aboriginal History*, 5 (1): 81–88.

Deveson, P. (2011) "The agency of the subject: Yolngu involvement in the Yirrkala Film Project," *Journal of Australian Studies*, 35 (2): 153–164.

Gibson, J., Angeles, S. and Liddle, J. (2019) "Deciphering the Arrernte archives," in Barwick, L., Green, J. and Vaarzan Morrel, P. (eds) *Language Documentation and Conservation*, Honolulu: University of Hawai'i Press.

Hamby, L. (2008) "Lloyd Warner: the reluctant collector," in Peterson, N., Hamby, L. and Allen, L. (eds) *Makers and Making of Indigenous Australian Museum Collections*, pp. 354–386, Melbourne: Melbourne University Press.

Jones, J. (2015) "A symphony of lines: reading south-east shields," in Sculthorpe, G., Carty, J., Morphy, H., Nugent, M., Coates, I., Bolton, L. and Jones, J. (eds) *Indigenous Australia: Enduring Civilisation*, pp. 74–78, London: British Museum Press.

Jones, P. (editor) (2017) *Gillen's Modest Record: his journal of the Spencer-Gillen anthropological expedition across Australia*, 1901–02, Adelaide: Friends of the State Library of South Australia.

McKenzie, K. (1980) *Waiting for Harry*, DVD, Canberra: Aboriginal Studies Press.

Morphy, F. and Morphy, H. (2006) "Tasting the waters: discriminating identities in the waters of Blue Mud Bay," *Journal of Material Culture*, 11 (1–2): 67–85.

Morphy, H. (2007) *Becoming Art: Exploring Cross-Cultural Categories*, Oxford: Berg.

Morphy, H. (2012) "Reading Spencer and Gillen," *Sophia*, 51 (4): 545–560.

Morphy, H. (2013) "Spencer at Oenpelli," in Hetherinton, M. (ed) *Glorious Days: Australia 1913*, pp. 159–168, Canberra: National Museum of Australia.

Mulvaney, J. (2008) "Annexing all I can lay my hands on," in Peterson, N., Hamby, L. and Allen, L. (eds) *Makers and Making of Indigenous Australian Museum Collections*, pp. 141–162, Melbourne: Melbourne University Press.

Mulvaney, J. and Calaby, J. (1985) *So Much That Is New – Baldwin Spencer 1860–1929, a Biography*, Melbourne: Melbourne University Press.

Nugent, M (2015) "Encounters in country," In Sculthorpe, G., Carty, J., Morphy, H., Nugent, M., Coates, I., Bolton, L. and Jones, J., *Indigenous Australia: Enduring Civilisation*, pp. 128–209, London: British Museum Press.

Nugent, M. and Sculthorpe, G. (2018) "A shield loaded with history: encounters, objects and exhibitions," *Australian Historical Studies*, 49 (1): 28–43.

Peterson, N., Allen, L. and Hamby, L. (eds) (2008) *The Makers and Making of Indigenous Australian Museum Collections*, Melbourne: Melbourne University Press.

Sayers, A. (1994) *Aboriginal Artists of the Nineteenth Century*, Melbourne: Oxford University Press in association with the National Gallery of Australia.

Spencer, W.B. (1928) *Wanderings in Wild Australia*, London: Macmillan.

Stanner, W.E.H. (1969) *After the Dreaming*, Sydney: Australian Broadcasting Corporation.

Stephen, A. (2017) "The oceanic primitivism of Len Lye's animation Tusalava (1929)," *Art History*, 40 (3).

Thomas, D. (2011) "Aboriginal art: who was interested?" *Journal of Art Historiography*, 4. http://arthistoriography.files.wordpress.com/2011/05/daniel-thomas-document.pdf.

von Zinnenburg Carroll, K. (2014) "The presence of absence: Tommy McRae and Judy Watson in *Australia*, the imaginary grandstand at the Royal Academy in London," *World Art*, 4 (2): 209–235.

West, M. (ed) (2008) *Yalangbara: The Art of the Djang'kawu*, Darwin: Charles Darwin University Press.

4 Contested values in the curation of human remains

Introduction

In this chapter, I will build on the distinction I have made between the two locals by looking at a key area of repatriation: that of human remains. In the context of Australia and the USA, the balance of power has on the surface shifted in favour of source communities. It could be argued indeed that legislatively, the issue has been solved in the USA by NAGPRA and in Australia by the Return of Indigenous Cultural Property programme. However, legislation masks the complexities of the issues involved and the fact that the return of human remains to communities is often just the first step in an ongoing process of engagement. The reasons for holding the collections in the first place cannot simply be dismissed as being of no account, in particular because human remains from other populations continue to be curated in institutional contexts and subject to the same research interests that existed before, albeit in a constantly changing social and ethical environment. In the Australian context, repatriation remains as much a topic of debate and public and media interest as it has ever been.

My focus is on the rights that different groups of people may claim in museum collections. These are embedded in ongoing dialogues between competing values, in dynamic value-creation processes, and entangled in debates about ethical decision making. The debate surrounding the issue of repatriation has been heated and at times polarizing. The theoretical discourse has often created a dualistic opposition or a set of oppositions between two groups of people, while at the same time aiming for a balanced outcome. Because the focus has been primarily on the rights of non-Western and Indigenous groups in collections in European or settler-colonial societies, the argument has often been phrased as an opposition between global Indigenous and non-Indigenous perspectives – for example, between those who believe in the continuing presence of the dead and those who do not (Dickerson and Ceeney 2015) and between humanistic perspectives and scientific views (see O'Sullivan 2012 for a relevant discussion).

Dickerson and Ceeney (2015: 93), in a general chapter on the ethics of repatriating human remains set up an opposition between the *dead-are-gone assumption* and the *dead-are-with-us assumption*. The former is the view that, 'those who are no longer living have no morally relevant interest in the contemporary polity', whilst the latter is the view that 'some of those who are no longer living are affected by the fate, actions and life-styles of their descendants, and thus have a morally relevant interest in the contemporary polity' (Mulgan 1999: 54).

The problem with many such generalizations created for heuristic purposes is that they essentialize different perspectives and reveal internal contradictions when applied to particular cases. It is clearly possible to believe that the dead have rights without believing that the dead are themselves affected by the actions of the living. There is also no necessary reason to assume that belief in the continuing presence of the dead is connected in one particular way to their physical remains. Beliefs about the relationship between spirit and body vary enormously across cultures, over time, and between religions. The polarization of the issues on the basis of religious beliefs also fails to account for more general changes in ethical standards and issues of informed individual consent that have developed in Western societies in recent decades, moving from best practice to the creation of legislative frameworks.[1]

While the issue of return of skeletal remains has been universalized in discourse as an exemplar of the problematic nature of museum collections, the reality is that the vast majority of human remains in institutions are not subject to claims for repatriation. The majority of human remains in the British Museum, for example, are from the British Isles, and the museum 'continues to acquire and hold certain human remains as part of research directed towards an increased understanding of the ancient and modern world' (Sculthorpe 2015: 33). Although the circumstances of collection and the associated cultural attitudes varies greatly 'for a small number of human remains, dialogues about whether the museum should continue to hold certain remains are likely to be ongoing'(ibid.). In a way, it is precisely because attitudes towards human remains vary so widely that discussion of their treatment provides an important context from which to examine how museums engage with the ethical issues. Established with a general remit to curate and conserve artefacts from across the world, for the benefit of future generations, how do or should museums engage with the ethical issues surrounding human remains?

Divergent interests within the academy

Lisa O'Sullivan, senior curator of medicine at the Science Museum, noted in a radio interview,

> Often it's quite embarrassing for a museum that's set up as a social history museum, that happens to have a nineteenth century skull, because that was seen as part of normal collecting practice at the time. So many museums have actually offered things back, however there are also collections which are still being actively used for research.[2]

Biological anthropologists and archaeologists, in particular those whose main concern is human evolution, may with some justification argue that they have not received the peer group support that they might have expected from other members of the anthropological community when it comes to formulating arguments and articulating the case against the return of skeletal material. One reason for this lack of support may be that, as anthropological objects, skeletal remains have been marginalized as a result of the historical position of biological anthropology within the broader discipline. Biological anthropology was for many years associated with that past era of nineteenth-century evolutionary anthropology, when artefacts, bones and cultural facts were to a certain extent subject to the same body of theory. Social and cultural anthropologists, particularly within the British tradition, struggled for years to disassociate their discipline from evolutionary theory but in so doing failed to keep up with the changes were taking place in the once closely allied discipline of biological anthropology. Biological anthropology has become, through no fault of its own, alienated from much of the remainder of anthropology and has become a victim of a stereotype that links it with a positivistic, invasive, and culturally insensitive approach to other cultures.

However, rather than conveniently treating human remains as someone else's problem, anthropologists would be well advised to see them as part of a much wider debate on anthropological knowledge. Defence of the validity of anthropological knowledge should be addressed from a broad perspective of common interest and research objectives across the discipline before making judgements on the particular issues. If the rights and interests of anthropologists and the subjects of their research are both to be recognized, then the rights of Indigenous people cannot be generalized to whatever emerges pragmatically as the most politically sensitive issue. Rights and interests must be developed on a broader basis of interaction and exchange of values and on a case by case basis, as the concerns of one community will not necessarily be shared by another. Decisions about the return of skeletal materials involve a balancing of different moral issues and diverse cultural values. This chapter is focussed on the curation of skeletal remains; however, it could as easily have addressed the return of sacred objects or rights in photographic images and pages of journals of exploration. Although there are fundamental differences between bones, objects, film, and field notes, it is not impossible to envisage circumstances in which the return of photographs, objects, and even writings could be a political issue as fraught as that of the return of skeletal material (see e.g. Willis 2008; Nugent and Sculthorpe 2018).[3]

I will begin by setting up an opposition between the rights of the museum (users and stakeholders) and the rights of the source communities or communities of origin. This polarization helps to articulate the issues and frames some of the broader arguments articulated by different museums and source communities. However, I will ultimately conclude that this polarization is misleading, since the professional museum community is increasingly composed of members of source communities (directors, curators, educators, and researchers) and source communities also provide outside stakeholders in the form of museum users, advisors, and collaborators.

Rights viewed from the perspective of the museum

The issue of the rights vested in museum objects is complex, and of necessity, I will limit myself to analyzing the ideology of public and university museums. I will not be concerned with the detailed legal position or with the case of private institutions. Museums are repositories of cultural knowledge in the form of objects. In the charter of most museums, the collections are inalienable and – except in special circumstances – objects are intended to be held forever. The collections should be available for research in order to contribute to the advance of knowledge in a particular field, and the museum should contribute to public education through exhibitions, public programmes, and publications. Thus objects in museums are public objects and a major set of rights in them is held on behalf of the community. The community is difficult to define precisely since it is an ideological construct mediated through the curators, trustees, and other higher authorities responsible for the management and legislation of the institution. It certainly includes more than those people with a research interest in the collections.

In abstract, the set of right holders in a 'global' or 'universal' museum is almost limitless in space and time. Although some museums are mainly of local interest or focus on national identity, many major museums have an international dimension. Most natural history and ethnographic museums, apart from showing national and historical biases in the structure of their collections, could be transported to any other museum-possessing culture and be of equal significance. Museums in this sense are international, and the museum curators in particular do not limit their services on the basis of the nationality of the client.

As far as time is concerned, museum curators deal with infinity on an almost routine basis. Light levels are set and storage conditions constructed to allow objects a maximum life span; the possibility of microscopic deterioration may be sufficient to prevent a loan or deny a researcher access to an object. Although in the case of a few objects, scientific storage conditions may well make it theoretically possible for them to outlast the human race, for the most part, the illusion of infinity is a conceit backed up by caution – the likely real duration of most of a museum's collections may be too depressingly short for words. Nonetheless, the 'infinity perspective' influences the view of who the stakeholders are, and the rights of a person living a century or more in the future have to be considered at the same time as those of the people who are living today. A consequence of such a broad perspective on rights may be that it diminishes the rights of those people who have the closest relationships to the objects concerned, or, rather, gives priority to rights – for example, rights of access – at such a general level that it diminishes the rights any particular group or person may wish to have. On the other hand, the wish of a particular group to destroy an object may be framed as a denial of the rights of future generations to have a say in the decision and to have access to the objects themselves. In a forthright article ironically titled 'Past Regained Future Lost', the archaeologist John Mulvaney comes to the heart of the matter when he writes, 'Can custodianship be logically equated with the right to destroy?' (Mulvaney 1991) Without making any judgement at this stage, any moral argument in favour of the destruction of objects should also take into account this responsibility for infinity, which museums see as one of their core reasons for existence.

Thus the justification for a museum's existence and the one without which such institutions would not exist is that it holds its collections for all times and makes them available for research.[4] Without this basis of understanding, people would not give objects to museums, and governments would not contribute to their running costs.

The rights from the perspective of the source community

The other set of rights relevant to the return of skeletal remains and sacred objects are the rights of the descendants, producers, and members of source communities. The legal rights of producers of museum objects vary enormously from country to country, depending on copyright legislation, moral rights, privacy laws, the protection of intellectual property and so on. The freedom to exhibit an artist's work as the curator sees fit is by no means universal. However, I am not concerned in this chapter with detailed legislation but with the general issues of the extent to which the descendants' wishes should be part of the curators' agenda: How would the producers wish their objects to be used and presented by others if their views were known? And, increasingly, how should the curator respond to their views or their descendants views when they are known? Such questions are part of the more general issue of the representation of other cultures, groups or persons and the use of information about them. Until 50 years ago, such issues were not at the top of the agenda of most museum curators. Museums, in particular ethnographic museums, tended to have a positivistic view of knowledge, and their collection policies and exhibitions were designed to present information about other cultures, their technology, their place in the history of mankind and the social context of their artefacts in an unproblematized and largely descriptive way.

Two things combined to undermine this traditional basis for, or ideology of, ethnographic museums and exhibitions: one was the growing recognition that such exhibitions were theory laden and influenced by underlying ideological assumptions, and the other was an increasing demand from Indigenous people, particularly the encapsulated fourth world peoples in countries such as Australia, Canada, and the USA to have a say in the way their cultures were being represented (Ames 1992; Kramer 2015). These two movements were interrelated, since the need to take account of the Indigenous response was often part of a theoretical critique that originated in the dominant society, and at the same time, the Indigenous response was one of the factors that changed the perceptions of the 'other' in the dominant societies.

There are in reality a multiplicity of Indigenous views, many of which are influenced by and are integrated within the political and ideological structures of dominant societies. However, this represents a complicating factor only if it is assumed that what ultimately needs to emerge is a single 'correct' view. The breakdown of a uniform positivist paradigm into a multiplicity of complementary perspectives should result in the recognition of multiple right holders, or relevant views, that have to be respected and responded to. The universality of the scientific paradigm comes into question; some of its underlying assumptions are questioned, but it remains a valid approach. The rights of the producers join in with the now fragmented interests of the consumers, as museums confront the reality of multiple audiences with conflicting demands. This fragmentation reflects the development of an increasingly complex view of culture in which it is recognized that objects and events are multiply determined and that their meaning varies greatly according to context and the position of the interpreter. Such a process of the opening up of the complexity of the world has at times been associated with a radical hermeneutic libertarianism in which everything is interpretation. I prefer to see fragmentation as reflecting the relativity of truth to the particular questions that are asked and the complexity of the social universe.[5] But in each case, truth has to be demonstrated in relation to the particular sets of assumptions and beliefs that produce it, and the complexity has to be recognized and elucidated.

How then do we accommodate the rights of producers or descendants? How do we rank them in relation to consumers, to curators, and to their audiences? In many cases, this can be done by responding to criticism by incorporating alternative perspectives within the same exhibition, by ensuring that subsequent exhibitions have alternative views represented, and so on. The real problem arises when one set of right holders demands are diametrically opposed to another's. This may occur where people say that their ancestors' bones should not only be removed from exhibition but returned to them for reburial or cremation.

Rights in skeletal material

Many museums, as O'Sullivan (2012) implied, could quite happily live with requests not to exhibit skeletal material and other human remains, even though there are, from their perspective, many valid reasons for doing so. The most contentious issue concerns the return of them to descendants, especially if the return is likely to result in their destruction. In the Australian Aboriginal case, activists and local communities have in some cases explicitly rejected compromises, such as storing the bones in keeping places where they can be preserved under Aboriginal custodianship, leaving open the possibility of future research.

Human skeletal remains are a major source of information for biological anthropologists about past lives; about people's diets, health, and the age structure of populations; and about the evolution, dispersal, and genetic relations between various human populations. Recent advances in analytic methods have exponentially increased the information potential of skeletal material, and there is no reason to suppose that such an increase will not continue. Macintosh and Larnach noted as early as the 1970s that skeletal remains from Australia are of immense scientific significance since they may represent the 'earliest examples of an evolving generalized modern *homo sapiens sapiens* to arrive in their ultimate area of migration' (1976: 124). Australian Pleistocene data are making a significant contribution to problems of human evolution in general, in particular around questions of the origins and dispersal of what are now referred to as modern humans. Recent research based on the analysis of mitochondrial DNA, as well as more traditional morphological analysis, has shown the rapid spread of modern humans and emphasized the genetic closeness of human populations outside Africa (Adcock et al. 2001; Webb 2018).

It is fair to say that research undertaken in Australia on human remains has transformed understanding of the human occupation of Australia and challenged previous assumptions. Perhaps the most important information flowed from the archaeological research undertaken at the Willandra Lakes in western New South Wales. Excavation at Lake Mungo had begun in 1967 after the geologist Jim Bowler discovered the cremated bones of a woman eroding out of a dune. Subsequent research dated her skeleton at some 42,000 years ago making it the world's oldest cremation and confirming an early date for the occupation of inland Australia. Several years later, the burial site of a male was excavated nearby with bones covered with red ochre. 'A picture was emerging that here, at a time when Europe was largely populated by Neanderthals, was an ancient culture of far more sophistication, full of symbolism with a thriving and complex belief system' (Westaway and Durban 2017: 3).

In the case of Australia, any well-documented skeletal material has the potential to produce useful information. Of particular importance are skeletal remains of known provenance and date. Any material from the immediate post-contact period can potentially provide information about genetic relations across Australia, biological or epidemiological correlates of particular forms of local organization, and data for comparing pre- and postcolonial populations on any number of dimensions. Thus Australian Aboriginal skeletal material is highly significant to human population studies, and with the development of new research techniques and methodologies, it is likely to provide increasingly more information.

The 'transcendent value' argument for keeping skeletal remains in museum custodianship in order to make them available for future generations of researchers is a very strong one. Yet in recent years, many collections have been returned to Aboriginal groups for reburial, including significant prehistoric collections, such the Kow Swamp burials of 9,000 to 15,000 years ago. Most recently, the remains from Mungo of 46,000 years ago have been returned to Indigenous custodianship. What were the counterarguments that enabled their return? What kind of moral arguments in favour of the rights of a narrow group of people can have the power to override the transcendent interests of science or 'world heritage'?

There are basically three arguments that have come to dominate repatriation discourses. The first is that the materials were illegally obtained against the wishes of the people concerned (Mansell 1985; Fforde et al. 2002). The second is that they are not the kind of objects that should ever be in museums since they are integral to the religious life of the community. Their presence in a museum is thus an act of sacrilege (Dickerson and Ceeney 2015).

The third argument is that research into skeletal remains is in theoretical terms opposed to the interests and beliefs of Aboriginal people, since in the past, it was associated with a racist ideology, which was integral to the European colonization of their land, and in the present, research generates theories of the population of Australia that run counter to the Dreamtime ideology of an autochthonous origin for Aboriginal people (see Mulvaney 1991: 19; Jenkins 2011). Clearly, elements of the different arguments can run together.

The context of collection

Although, in many cases, there is no direct evidence that the human remains were obtained against Aboriginal wishes, this may be because the material itself is so badly documented. In many better documented cases, the material was excavated from archaeological contexts, and until 40 years ago, such excavation rarely involved consultation with Aboriginal people. In the majority of cases, then, it is reasonable to assume that the human remains were collected without the consent of Aboriginal people. There are, moreover, a number of notorious cases in which we know that they were removed against the explicit wishes of the people concerned.

The most difficult argument to counter, yet also, in some ways, to substantiate, is the general one that the colonial nature of the relationship between Indigenous people and Europeans meant that, inevitably, anything obtained by museums was a product of the dominance by Europeans of the Aboriginal population and hence not freely given. Such an argument applies equally to skeletal and non-skeletal materials and can be extended to words as well as things, and addressing this is one of the central themes of this book. It is vital to examine the circumstances and history of collections and to be conscious of the differential power relationships that existed at the time they were made. However, it is also possible to exaggerate the extent to which museum objects are the products of domination – indeed, a good argument can be made that in many cases, they are the products of Aboriginal resistance. As we saw in Chapter 3, many of the Aboriginal objects in museum collections are there as the result of attempts by Aboriginal people to exchange ideas, to develop economic relations and, more generally, to attempt to engage the European other. Seeing objects in museum collections as signs of the colonial domination of Aboriginal society rather than as assertions of Aboriginal values in alien contexts risks interpreting the evidence too narrowly.

The argument that the way something was obtained affects moral rights in it is a strong one, though it is clearly not going to be decisive in all cases. The case is almost unanswerable in parts of southern Australia, including

Tasmania, where Aboriginal populations were decimated through disease and murder and the generally debilitating conditions of colonization. The human remains in the museums must, in many cases, have been the skeletons of known individuals placed there against their wishes. To their descendants, they inevitably became a symbol of the colonial encounter and of the domination of Aboriginal people by the colonists, the appropriation of their land and the threat to their identity and continued survival.

A key question that arises is how far back in time should such moral rights be extended. The further back in time we go, the harder it becomes to know the circumstances of the death or to establish relationships with living people. It is in such cases that the issue has become most contested: should the rights in the remains be vested in humanity as a whole – transcendent rights, the skeletal equivalent of world cultural heritage – or should the rights be vested in the Indigenous group local to the area where the bones have been excavated?

In such contexts, it is desirable, if at all possible, for the interests of both sets of right holders to be recognized and taken into account in any decisions that are eventually made. The relative balance of rights shifts over time in two ways: one is the time that has elapsed since the death, the other is the time over which debate between the Indigenous and the scientific communities has developed (Dolan 2001). The cases of the bones of known people, cases where the material has been stolen or illegally obtained, are ones in which it is hard to imagine Indigenous rights not being given priority. In Tasmania and some other areas of Australia, the analogy with the Holocaust is inescapable. In the case of ancient prehistoric materials, the balance is much less clear; the extent to which sentiments are shared between the competing claimants and the general population is going to be a significant factor in determining the outcome. It is likely that the sentiments of Indigenous and non-Indigenous Australians today will coincide in the case of human remains that can be thought of as closely related ancestors of contemporary populations. However, coincidence of opinion is less likely in the case of human remains that are thought to represent much earlier populations. As John Mulvaney has argued, the French are proud of their Palaeolithic heritage and would not welcome its destruction.

In this context, it is relevant to reflect on the fate of the European man whose mummified body was discovered encased in ice in an Alpine glacier on the Austrian-Italian border. He was named Ötzi, after the mountain range. He was discovered in 1991 by two tourists who at first assumed that it was the body of a mountaineer. His body was recovered from the ice, and it became clear from his clothing and weapons that he came from an earlier era. The remains were and continue to be subject to scientific research and analysis. He died some 5,300 years ago as result of an arrow wound.

Ownership of the remains was contested. The body was discovered on the border between Austria and Italy, and it was necessary to determine which country held jurisdiction over it. Surveys of the site showed that he lay 92.56 metres on the Italian side of the border. The South Tyrol claimed property rights but agreed to let the University of Innsbruck in Austria continue its scientific examinations. The second dispute was less amicably settled and involved a legal case to determine who would benefit from the 'finders' fee for Ötzi's body under Italian law.

Ötzi's body was eventually moved from Innsbruck to be placed in the South Tyrol Museum of Archaeology, which was established in Bolzano for that primary purpose. His body is conserved in a climate-controlled chamber within the museum at a temperature of −6 Celsius and 98% humidity, replicating glacier conditions in which it was found. The museum, through cultural tourism, is an important component of the local economy as well as being a focal point for regional archaeology. Ötzi and other mummified remains from elsewhere in Europe are not isolated from issues of respect for the remains for the dead and attitudes toward the exhibition of human remains. Curation of the bodies from the Iron Age preserved in peat bogs in England, Ireland, and Germany have caused institutions to reflect deeply on the balance between knowledge, wonder, curiosity, respect, and belief in curating, researching, and exhibiting such finds. But as public institutions in diverse societies, they have attempted to accommodate the existence of very different attitudes among the broader community of museumgoers, while enabling that diversity to be expressed.

Religious beliefs and spiritual identity

The second grounds for reclaiming skeletal material are religious beliefs. A wide range of mortuary practices once existed throughout Australia, but in many areas, the disposal of the bones of the dead was an integral part of religious practice. In much of northern Australia, burial rites took place over a number of years, and the final return of the bones to the land was taken as a sign of the return of the spirit to the spirit domain – bones were considered a sacred part of the person and seen as representing the permanent foundation of the clan. Even today, when secondary and tertiary burial are rarely practised, the structure and themes of mortuary rituals remain similar with possessions and memorial posts substituting on occasion for the absent body. The initial and final burial of the body in a grave reflects an adjustment to European customs and sensibilities rather than a radical discontinuity with previous practice.[6] In much of southern Australia, where the demand for the return of skeletal material has been strongest, the change in practice has been greatest, often resulting in a predominantly Christian burial of the dead. Memories of pre-contact mortuary practices are in many cases mediated by people from a literate tradition with access to early anthropological accounts as well as oral histories. In a contemporary context, archival sources and the results of archaeological research need to be acknowledged as components of people's understanding of self.

Anthropologists should be the first to recognize that human societies are in a continual state of change, and continuities are created as much out of the present as out of past practices. Details of immediate post-contact practices are at one level quite irrelevant to the religious sentiments of the present, and there is no reason why people should not believe that the fate of the past soul depends on the return of the individual's bones to the land. Christian influence should not make it less reasonable for Aboriginal people to wish the body to be returned to the grave, even if some Christians believe, as do some Arnhem Landers, that once the soul has left, the bones are no longer an integral part of the individual. The difficulty that anthropologists face is that coming from a tradition that is at the same time scientific and relativistic, whose practitioners are generally tolerant of other peoples' beliefs since they are trained to suspend their own, they find it difficult to confront fundamentalism in any form. This is particularly true when the fundamentalist argument comes from those whose beliefs they have previously been defending. Ironically, accepting the fact that people will change, and acknowledging peoples' right to change, does not in itself solve the problem of competing rights. Rather, it compounds the problem since the descendants of contemporary populations may hold quite different views than the present generations. From this perspective, it is quite logical that John Mulvaney should have been outraged by the fundamentalism of some Aboriginal advocates for the return and destruction of skeletal material – not only on scientific grounds but also on the grounds that they are denying their descendants future possibilities.

Colonial science

The third set of arguments in favour of the return of skeletal material are against the research itself, either in relation to the history of biological anthropology or its present-day objectives. Much nineteenth-century biological science was concerned with the identification of racial types and with the relative position of those types on the ladder of human evolution. The practice and perhaps even more so the style of this nineteenth-century research often appeared to treat both dead and living members of other cultures as inferior objects of research, certainly not as equal partners in the quest for human origins. Many of the negative connotations of biological anthropological practice – that still have currency – may be a consequence of the natural and cultural symbolism of the human skulls in their ordered ranks in the anatomist's ossuary. Such displays, as well as being signs of the objectification that is one of the consequences of the scientific approach, hint at skulls as trophies held by victors, symbols of the appropriation of the power of others. In the case of the practitioners themselves, a certain distancing from the humanity of the subjects by treating the skeletal remains as scientific specimens to be filed in ordered sets according to classificatory principles may be necessary in order to avoid confronting the question of mortality at every step, to make the enterprise like any other in evolutionary science, with humans being no different from any other animal. The psychological distancing of the scientist may be a precise complement to the closeness felt by the descendants – the former avoiding the death of the subject and the latter focussing on it.[7]

It is particularly frustrating for today's biological anthropologists to be tarred by the brush of their nineteenth-century predecessors. Recent research has often had the effect of disproving racist theoretical assumptions and has provided valuable ammunition for Aboriginal people to use in defence of their rights and to achieve recognition for their cultural heritage.

Twentieth-century archaeologists and biological anthropologists have demonstrated the antiquity of people in Australia, their contribution to human cultural development, and their genetic closeness to, for example, the populations of northern Europe – in other words, they have demonstrated both their uniqueness and their equality, two of the essential points that Aboriginal people themselves have been making. This does not in any way justify the appalling way in which much of the material was obtained in the past, but it does place the motivations of the researchers of today in a very different light.

Different ontologies

The argument that Western science has been involved in attitudinal change is sometimes countered by noting that the requirement to make a defence in such terms is in itself a consequence of colonialism, and even by putting forward positive arguments within that framework, anthropologists and archaeologists are acting as agents of the continuing colonial process. It is in this context that some have argued that any demonstration of the common origins of humankind is against Aboriginal beliefs. Many of the Aboriginal activists who are demanding the return of skeletal material argue, at least in public, for a Dreamtime or independent origin for the Aboriginal population.[8]

According to such belief, the genesis of the different Aboriginal groups was in the different parts of Australia where they live today. They were created by the Dreamtime ancestors who created their land. This process of Dreamtime creation continues into the present. The present and the past are linked in a cyclical process whereby each child is the product of spirit conception that directly links him or her in with the Dreaming. Very often, this process of Dreamtime creation also involves the recycling of the souls of the dead, which is accomplished largely through correct burial practice. From this perspective, and combining concern for the fate of the individual's soul with requirements of group survival, people could feel deep unease at the thought of skeletons of relatives, however distant, remaining forever in remote museums. People may feel deep sorrow for the person whose sacred journey has been deflected or suspended while his or her remains are locked behind a succession of glass showcases or joins the ranks of those stored on the shelves of the museum basement, and they could feel the loss of a spiritual resource.

I do not intend this to be anything more than a story of how a group of contemporary Aboriginal people might feel, as something that could flow logically out of some sets of classical Aboriginal beliefs. Many people are not going to have this reaction. Certainly, I have no evidence that the people of northeast Arnhem Land, who hold most of the beliefs that I outlined earlier, were in any way deeply concerned about relatives whose skeletal remains were held in Australian museum collections. In the past, once the mortuary cycle had been completed and the bones were broken up and placed in a hollow log coffin, they were viewed as spiritually relatively inert but deeply imbricated in the memory of the deceased. Any removal without consent would be intolerable.

What I hope I have shown is not how the request for the return of skeletal remains comes out of a common set of Aboriginal beliefs, which is certainly not the case, but how a whole variety of factors operates together to make it likely that the return of skeletal material in some cases, and in some contexts, will strike a strong chord among many different groups of Aboriginal people, depending on their particular history, the history of the skeletal material concerned, and contemporary political context. I hope I have shown why arguments directed towards particular counterarguments cannot easily work when what one is concerned with is a whole climate of opinion.

Arguments against the return of skeletal material

What then are the strongest arguments that can be employed in favour of the retention of skeletal material? Essentially, they are the arguments that we have summarized already and the arguments of general principle that have been put forward by scientists. John Mulvaney's argument against fundamentalism is a strong one, as is the implicit argument in favour of academic freedom and against the censorship of history, but they are essentially arguments from the point of view of the transcendence of science. In order to be accepted, they require persuasion, for they are up against the beliefs, the grievances, and the emotions of the present and the rights of particular individuals and groups. It is clearly vital that arguments be put forward in favour of the research objectives, even while conceding the moral argument in favour of the return of skeletal material in particular cases. It is necessary to challenge the misconceptions about the nature of research, its objectives, and the moral and ethical stance of the scientific community. It is important to disabuse people of the idea that the present objectives are closely allied to the idea of nineteenth-century racist theorists. The danger of returning material without clarifying the basis on which it is being returned is that it may be taken as a tacit acceptance that all of these ideas are valid – arguments that can be applied just as easily to many other areas of anthropology.

If museums are holding things on behalf of science and humanity at large, the solution must be to involve the producers, owners, and descendants in the curation of the collections and in the decision-making process. This does not mean the immediate handing over of control but rather the development of partnerships – reinforcing the ideology that a museum has multiple audiences and multiple right holders and that a museum conserves things for research, knowledge creation, and as a record of human creativity and the history of the world. But just as this provides a moral justification for the custodianship of other people's material culture, it also creates a moral obligation to include those people among the body of decision makers.[9]

The arguments over the return of skeletal materials are largely about the value that objects have to people and in interactions among people. It is inevitable that values will differ according to peoples' relative positions in the historical process and where in their trajectories through life particular objects are placed. If we are part of a world community, then it has to be in spite of this conflict over values. It cannot mean that we all have to think the same way since that would almost inevitably mean the imposition of a hegemony of values onto a world system. It means that we must allow for and respect the existence of deeply held views that are fundamental to peoples' senses of identity, yet it also means that those views exist in the context of a discourse in which other publics have rights. We are all actively involved in an engagement over the value and meaning of objects – laying claims over them for purposes that are often temporary in the case of objects whose future is unknown and whose potential largely untapped. As Chris Anderson wrote, at the time he was responsible at the South Australian Museum for the curation and in some cases repatriation of sacred objects from the collections,

> There can be neither moral nor political content in a relationship between groups that do not know each other, which has therefore no

> social substance. If we want to do things according to Aboriginal tradition, then it is not simply a moral and political response, which is required in cases of repatriation. An alternative way of looking at such transfers is to consider objects as part of a dynamic social/ceremonial/political and economic system, in which objects circulate, and create sets of rights and obligations between individuals and groups or institutions. In other words the objects act as social currency.
>
> (1990: 54–55)

While it could be argued that this is simply involving Aboriginal people in the culture of the museums as a means of subverting their resistance, it could also be seen as a transformation of the concept of the museum through its incorporation of Indigenous concepts. It is certainly the case that Anderson sees such developments as resulting in the mutual understanding of each other's motives and objectives and in a forum being created for the exchange of value. One of the ideas communicated will clearly be the concept of the transcendent value of particular categories of museum objects. The justification of preservation for future populations is a very strong one, but it is not an absolute one. And at least for moments in time, the value of holding an object in a museum may become so negative that the pressures to release it can appear to be overwhelming.

The frustration of many Australian prehistorians and biological anthropologists about the involvement of political institutions in the return of prehistoric skeletal materials is understandable. The dialogue between Aboriginal Australians and museums and the associated professions has developed productively over the past 20 years. Involvement of Aboriginal communities and individuals in research has become substantial. Permission of relevant groups is sought before any excavations are carried out; Aboriginal interests are considered in developing research proposals; many Indigenous people have become professionals in anthropology, archaeology, and museum curation. Structures to enable Aboriginal involvement in the management of collections and in collection policy now exist, and the development of keeping houses in local communities has created the possibility for Aboriginal groups to hold sensitive materials under their own custodianship.

In an article examining the response to the Museums Australia policy document *Previous Possessions New Obligations*, Dolan (2001) pointed out the sense of powerlessness felt by many museum professionals when faced with government and policy. All things being equal, the struggle over the value and destiny of objects is likely to be a tough one, punctuated by disputes in which neither side is prepared to give way, and confrontations where each side is going to prove authoritarian to the other. Both sides are not equal, and there is a heavy irony underlying the relationship. On the one hand, the history of colonial domination and the present poverty of much of the Aboriginal population makes it likely that many Aboriginal political activists will reject the universalistic and transcendent arguments of the scientist as a matter of principle. On the other hand, politicians will support Aboriginal demands on pragmatic grounds and perhaps on the basis of sensitivities and attitudes towards their 'own' mortal remains. Aboriginal people have relatively little power, but the same is true of museum curators. In the latter part of the twentieth century, many museums moved from a time in which their Indigenous collections were largely disconnected from the communities of origin to one in which, under some jurisdictions, the legal right of return of human remains was recognized. The movement that enabled this transformation was located in museum discourse as much as in the world outside, and it was associated in some cases with changes in the relationships between the museums and the communities they answered to (Karp et al. 1992).

Chips Colwell (2017: 267), writing about the analogous context of human remains in the USA, argues that by developing positive relationships, the interests of researchers and Indigenous communities can often be accommodated. He contrasts the case of Kennewick Man whose 9,300-year-old remains were uncovered in Washington in 1996 with a skeleton, older by 1,000 years, discovered at On Your Knees Cave in Alaska in the same year. The Kennewick case was a highly contested one and placed the research in a hostile environment. In contrast, the scientists involved in researching the On Your Knees remains from the beginning developed a collaborative relationship with the local Tlingit community organizations, and through a 12-year partnership, the human remains were fully studied and published with the consent of the native peoples. But such processes are always going to be complex and negotiated.

Returning to Mungo

Maria Nugent covers the complexities of the Mungo case when she states that Mungo woman

> embodies' both the deepest claim to deep time and continuity, as well as being a 'thing' around which many other contemporary and changing claims accrue. At the same time, she might also work to displace or overshadow other claims.
>
> (Kennedy et al. 2016: 258)

The cremated remains of Mungo Lady, scattered with red ochre, were uncovered by the geologist Jim Bowler in 1968 on the shores of a lake basin on a

Mungo sheep station in western New South Wales while he was conducting research on climate change. Bowler continued his research on the regional geology, and in 1974, after heavy rain, he saw the top of a skull eroding out of one of the dunes. The body was buried in a flexed position and specks of ochre showed evidence of ritual practice. This was Mungo Man. The excavation was led by Alan Thorne of the Australian National University, and the subsequent research on the remains was carried out at the ANU. The burial was eventually dated at 43,000 years. The geomorphology and environment of the Willandra Lakes region has meant that momentary events in past lives are preserved beneath the surface of the dunes – a single meal around a fire, an overnight camp, a cremation, and a burial. In 2003, sets of 2,000-year-old footprints were found embedded in a nearby clay pan (Webb et al. 2006). The immediacy of the past is palpable.

Mungo Lady was discovered just at the moment that Australian archaeology was beginning to take a lead in engaging with local communities and putting in place best practice codes that in some cases eventually became the basis of legislation. The theoretical focus of Australian archaeology was on the longue durée. While it can be argued that seeking early dates is an essential part of the mystique of archaeology, it was also directed towards establishing the duration of Aboriginal occupation of Australia and the sophisticated nature of the relationship between people and the environment. 'The oldest living culture of the world' was not positioning Aboriginal people as a relic from the past but as a way of life that had continued into the present through a long-term engagement with the Australian environment.

The remains of Mungo Lady and Mungo Man were originally housed at the ANU, and their management became increasingly collaborative. Alan Thorne negotiated the repatriation of the remains of Mungo Lady in 1992. Responsibility for the collection as a whole was placed in a joint management committee made up equally of Aboriginal community members and non-Indigenous representatives. The committee was involved in the decision-making processes in all subsequent research, which has meant that relatively little research has actually been undertaken over the past 30 years (Westaway and Durban 2017). The research undertaken at Mungo has had a major impact nationally and internationally. On the National Museum's website, Mungo Man's discovery is referred to as one of the defining moments in Australia's history. The archaeological research in the region was a major factor in the recognition of Willandra Lakes as a UNESCO world heritage area in 1981, jointly managed by the New South Wales National Parks and Wildlife Service and the traditional owners group comprising representatives of the Mutthi Mutthi, Ngiyampaa, and Paakantji peoples.

Over the years following the initial excavations, government legislation conferred the rights in human remains to the local Indigenous community.

In 2014, the joint management group was dissolved, and on the 40th anniversary of the discovery of Mungo Lady, the traditional owners of the Willandra Lakes region requested that the entire Mungo collection be returned. As an interim measure while people prepared for its return, the collection was transferred to the National Museum of Australia. In November 2017, the remains were finally returned to Lake Mungo in a major ceremonial event.

Response to the return of the Mungo remains has brought to the fore many of the issue involved from the perspectives of both the Indigenous community and of the broader academy. In the case of the traditional owners, there was a sense that it was time for the remains to return home, yet at the same time, being away had been productive. Talking of Mungo Lady, Gary Pappin says, 'She gave us a voice and we're using it' (Kennedy et al. 2016: 253).

James Grubel (2014) interviewed Mutthi Mutthi elder Mary Pappin at the ceremony marking the temporary transfer of the Mungo remains from the ANU to the National Museum. He reported,

> She wants Mungo Man's repatriation to the Willandra Lakes to be a unifying moment for all Indigenous Australians and a great celebration of Mungo Man's role in establishing a continuous Indigenous culture dating back 40,000 years. 'He's a remarkable person that Mungo Man. . . . But he's done his job. It's time for him to go and rest now'.

On the final return to Mungo, Miki Perkins (2017) interviewed Paakantyi elder Warren Clark, who she reports said,

> If he'd known about the discovery of Mungo Man at the time, [he] wouldn't have agreed it should be taken away for research. But he also believes the scientific insight into his people's cultural longevity has value: 'Now we have this information, we can walk together on these human lands.'

And in an article in the *Guardian* reflecting on his involvement over the years, Jim Bowler quoted Mary Pappin's admonition: 'You did not find Mungo Lady and Mungo Man – they found you!'

The archaeologists, conservators, and curators who worked on the Mungo remains over a period of some 40 years had a positive and at the same time uneasy relationship with the community. Early on, they recognized and respected the rights and interests of the community ahead of any legislative changes. They saw themselves engaged in a value-creation process at a time of attitudinal change in Australia in which the wrongs of history were increasingly being acknowledged and attempts were being made to remedy them in the present. Bowler's (2014) metaphors at times even echo those of the elders: 'In emerging from that grave Mungo Man continues to challenge ignorance and prejudice'. But at the same time, the archaeologists could be seen by the local community as representing that past history, even as they believed that the work that they were engaged in could be made compatible with the diversity of Indigenous interests and conflicting beliefs. They could be seen to be active parties in a new frontier that existed in continuity with the past.

This dual positioning of the archaeologists is also reflected in some areas of academic discourse. In a discussion of a film she and Andrew Pike made with a focus on Mungo Lady, Ann McGrath says,

> It is the scientists that are coming in as 'outsiders'. They are part of the whole colonial system and they are part of the imperial knowledge system. They're representing not just Australian nationalism, but the universal belief in Western science that delivers so much confidence and prestige. To make an amazing discovery that goes back a really long way delivers much kudos. So there's a complex value system that's different from the local value system.
>
> (Kennedy et al. 2016: 253)

Interestingly, when focussing on redemption, the archaeologists are again singled out as representatives of the past. Rosanne Kennedy noted, 'For me the return of Mungo Lady felt like it was a redemptive moment for white scientists' (ibid. 2016: 256). Ann McGrath (ibid. 2016: 257) followed this up by suggesting that

> because of the power of Alan Thorne's redemption story, some other scientists are now trying to cut in and have a share of the cake – the redemption cake. Once science in the area was about the prestige of discovery and now there's the prestige of return.

Conclusion

The remains of Mungo Lady and Mungo Man are presently being held in a secure location in the national park. An Aboriginal advisory group made up of members from three traditional owner groups of the Willandra Lakes Regional World Heritage Area – the Mutthi Mutthi, Ngiyampaa, and Paakantji – is currently tasked with providing advice on managing the area. The decision as to what will become of the remains is vested in the Indigenous 'community', but as with any community, it contains within it people with very different ideas who represent many different interests. Some people want the remains to be reburied while others want them to be conserved. In many ways, the dilemmas that confront the Indigenous community overlap and are entangled with those of the museum community. The return of the remains does not resolve the issue for the source community, but it does give them the major responsibility for finding the solution.

In an article in the *National Indigenous Times* on the 25 July 2018, under the headline 'Leaders Call for United Action on Mungo', the National Congress of Australia's First People, acknowledging that the remains had been returned to Mungo, argued that the government should in the words of co-chair Rod Little provide 'a national keeping place that has the proper temperature control facility'. He continued,

> If the government can spend a hundred million dollars on a war memorial in France or somewhere like that then surely they could spend the same amount of money on a keeping place for First Peoples because we are a part of this continent's history and that needs to be recognized and valued.

While Little is not calling for the building of the kind of institution that houses Ötzi's body in Bolzano, he is reflecting on the failure of governments to provide the resources that would give options for the local community in the Willandra Lakes to explore different ways of respectfully returning Mungo Lady and Mungo Man to their place.

The dialogue between Indigenous Australians and museums and their associated professions has developed productively over the past 40 years. Involvement of Aboriginal people in research has become substantial. These very processes of dialogue and exchange, together with the acknowledgement of an increasingly broad range of interest in museum collections, are themselves part of value-creation processes that change understandings of the world. They set the basis for understanding Indigenous views on museum collections and equally the different ways in which those collections are valued and perceived in society more generally. That dialogue and the increased representation of Indigenous people in the work of museums is likely to change Indigenous understandings of the value potential and connotations of museum collections. The fear among many curators is that the instrument of law and directive government policy, set up in an atmosphere of conflict and mutual distrust, cuts across dialogues that may require time to evolve productively. The law may intervene to call a halt to processes of persuasion that are ongoing and are achieving successful outcomes in more local arenas. The boundaries between the unanswerable cases for the return of skeletal material and the cases where the demand has not even been articulated may be blurred. In the blurred boundary zone, the variety of opinions among contemporary the Aboriginal population and the choices of future generations of Aboriginal people needs to be included within the wider discourse. Ultimately, infinity belongs to no one in particular and is of no particular time.

Notes

1 Jenkins (2011: 29ff.) explores the connection between controversies over the use of body parts in medical research without consent and the repatriation of human remains to indigenous communities.
2 ABC Radio National Rear Vision 12 August 2009 *Regarding Human Remains*.
3 Bolton (2015: 230) has argued that 'the human remains issue has made moral and emotional considerations acceptable as a reason to return objects – and moral impetus now has considerable power [and that] . . . most accounts of repatriation are essentially celebratory'.
4 Clearly, the two functions can sometimes be in conflict – for example, in the case of objects that are so fragile that access to them has to be severely limited or objects that are so politically or culturally sensitive that access has to be restricted.
5 Tiffany Jenkins (2012, Chapter 6) tackles this in her analysis of the 2008–2009 exhibition at the Manchester Museum of Lindow man whose body was preserved in a peat bog in the north of England. Research had centred on what it was possible to learn about his life and times, and that had been the primary focus of previous exhibitions. The Manchester exhibition aimed to problematize that approach by adopting a pluralist approach which gave equal weight to different interpretations and challenged the presumed more distanced approach of archaeology.
6 For details of Yolngu mortuary practice and their relationship to religion and the fate of the soul, see Morphy and Morphy (2012).
7 Jenkins provides a detailed discussion of this topic and rhetoric of repatriation.
8 There is, of course, no reason why some Aboriginal theologian or theological process should not make a belief in a common origin for humanity and a unique origin through spirit conception compatible.
9 This position was clearly articulated by the path-breaking report by the Council of Australian Museum Associations, *Previous Possessions New Obligations: Policies for Museums in Australia and Aboriginal and Torres Strait Islander Peoples*.

References

Adcock, G., Dennis, E., Easteal, S., Huttley, G., Jermiin, L., Peacock, W.J. and Thorne, A. (2001) "Mitochondrial DNA sequences in ancient Australians: implications for modern human origins," *Proceedings of the National Academy of Sciences of the U S A*, 98 (2): 537–542.

Ames, M. (1992) *Cannibal Tours and Glass Boxes*, Vancouver: UBC Press.

Anderson, C. (1990) "Repatriation of cultural property: a social process," *Museum*, 165 (1): 54–55.

Bolton, L. (2015) "An ethnography of repatriation: engagements with Erromango, Vanuatu," in Coombes, A.E. and Phillips, R.P. (eds) *Museum Transformations: Art, Culture, History*, pp. 229–248, Oxford: Wiley Blackwell.

Bowler, J. (2014) "Mungo Man is a physical reminder for Indigenous recognition," *The Guardian*, 25 February. www.theguardian.com/world/2014/feb/25/mungo-man-physical-reminder-need-for-indigenous-recognition.

Colwell, C. (2017) *Plundered Skulls and Stolen Spirits*, Chicago: University of Chicago Press.

Dickerson, A. and Ceeney, E. (2015) "Repatriating human remains: searching for an acceptable ethics," in Ireland, T. and Schofield, J. (eds) *The Ethics of Cultural Heritage*, pp. 89–104, New York: Springer.

Dolan, J. (2001) "Making policy practice: previous possessions new obligations in western Australian community museums," *Open Museum Journal*, 3: 1–27.

Fforde, C., Hubert, J. and Turnbull, P. (eds) (2002) *The Dead and Their Possessions: Repatriation in Principle, Policy and Practice*, London: Routledge.

Grubel, J. (2014) "Mungo Man's long journey back to country," *ANU Reporter*, 47 (1). https://reporter.anu.edu.au/mungo-man's-long-journey-back-country.

Jenkins, T. (2011) *Contesting Human Remains in Museum Collections: The Crisis of Cultural Authority*, Abingdon: Routledge.

Karp, I., Kreamer, C. and Lavine, S. (eds) (1992) *Museums and Communities: The Politics of Public Culture*, Washington: The Smithsonian Institution Press.

Kennedy, R., Leane, J., McGrath, A., Moore, N. and Nugent, M. (2016) "Roundtable: *message from Mungo* and the scales of memory," *Australian Humanities Review*, 59: 247–258.

Kramer, J. (2015) "Möbius museology," in Coombs, A. and Phillips, R. (eds) *International Handbook of Museums: Museum Transformations*, pp. 489–510, Chichester: Wiley Blackwell.

Macintosh, N.W.G. and Larnach, S.L. (1976) "Aboriginal affinities looked at in the world context," in Kirk, R.L. and Thorne, A.G. (eds) *The Origin of the Australians*, pp. 113–126, Canberra: Australian Institute of Aboriginal Studies.

Mansell, M. (1985) "Tasmanian aboriginal bones," *Anthropology Today*, 1 (6): 27.

Morphy, F. and Morphy, H. (2012) "Soon we will be spending all our time at funerals," in Howe, S. and Talle, A. (eds) *Returns to the Field*, pp. 49–72, Bloomington: Indiana University Press.

Mulgan, T. (1999) "The place of the dead in liberal political philosophy," *Journal of Political Philosophy*, 7 (1): 52–70.

Mulvaney, J. (1991) "Past regained future lost: the Kow Swamp Pleistocene burials," *Antiquity*, 65 (246): 12–21.

Nugent, M. and Sculthorpe, G. (2018) "A shield loaded with history: encounters, objects and exhibitions," *Australian Historical Studies*, 49 (1): 28–43.

O'Sullivan, L. (2012) "Material legacies: indigenous remains and contested values in UK museum collections," *Cross/Cultures*, 151: 391–493.

Perkins, M. (2017) "The long way: fire and smoke for Mungo Man and the ancestors on their road home," *The Age*, 16 November. www.theage.com.au/national/victoria/the-long-way-fire-and-smoke-for-mungo-man-and-the-ancestors-on-their-road-home-20171116-gzn45a.html.

Sculthorpe, G. (2015) "Caring for, conserving and storing human remains," in Fletcher, A., Antoine, D. and Hill, J.D. (eds) *Regarding the Dead: Human Remains in the British Museum*, pp. 31–34, London: British Museum Press.

Webb, S. (2018) *Made in Africa: Hominin Explorations and the Australian Skeletal Evidence*, San Diego: Academic Press.

Webb, S., Cupper, M. and Robins, R. (2006) "Pleistocene human footprints from the Willandra Lakes, Southeastern Australia," *Journal of Human Evolution*, 50: 405–413.

Westaway, M. and Durband, A. (2017) "Mungo Man returns home: there is still much he can teach us about ancient Australia," *The Conversation*, 15 November. http://theconversation.com/mungo-man-returns-home-there-is-still-much-he-can-teach-us-about-ancient-australia-87264.

Willis, E. (2008) "The law, politics, and 'historical wounds': the Dja Dja Wurrung bark etchings case in Australia," *International Journal of Cultural Property*, 15 (1): 49–63.

5 Open access versus the culture of protocols

This book is primarily centred on ethnographic collections of non-Western material culture that have been housed in Western institutions. From a European perspective, research and collections have been integral to value-creation processes that have changed Western views and understandings of the diversity of world cultures. Other cultures have been equally involved, creating cross-cultural understandings through processes of trade and exchange, diplomacy, and migration. Other societies have built and conserved collections on varying scales and with different purposes. We can set the royal palaces of Europe alongside the sacra of the house *tambarans* of Papua New Guinea, the archives and religious artefacts of Egypt, the courthouses of African Kingdoms, and the temples of Tibet. But museums and collections, as primarily cultural, educational, and research institutions, developed in post-Enlightenment Europe before becoming characteristic of nation-states on a more global basis.

The presence of collections in museums in Europe and America is a sign of the high esteem in which they were held. They are the material evidence of an educational process that changed attitudes, and they are a continuing and potentially expanding resource. The value of the collections has changed as appreciation of the richness of cultural production in other places and times has grown and as people have become more receptive to non-Western forms of music, art, and poetry. The collections, however, have primarily been embedded in a Western discourse, and issues of access have centred on making them and associated archival resources available to Western-based researchers and educationalists. The issue of access to collections by members of source communities, of the cultures of production, has not until now been a primary concern. The collections have not been seen as a community resource for the cultures of production. This applies to all collections not just to ethnographic collections, but as I have argued in the preceding chapters, collections that were made from societies during periods of colonial rule have a particular salience. The archives, objects, and images have often been doubly disconnected from the cultures of origin – disconnected in time but also disconnected in the sense that they are no longer an integral part of the activities of the societies concerned. Hence reengagement with the material is likely to involve a dual process of discovery and meaningful reconnection.

The majority of items in museum collections were trade items, and the majority of archival resources, photographs, and sound and film recordings in museums and archives were obtained by people who had established positive relationships with the producers. The nature of these relationships was often well ahead of its time, but of that time, and needed to be placed in that context. Since the end of the nineteenth century at least, some members of source communities have been actively involved in the building of collections, and collections are being added to in the present, often seen as a desired destination from the perspective of the makers. However, irrespective of the context of collection, material objects traded in the eighteenth, nineteenth, and early twentieth centuries have become scarce resources and knowledge of where they are held has often been lost.

It could be argued that loss is an integral part of social and cultural change. Past technologies cease to be relevant to present ways of life, and the skills associated with them are no longer practised. Religious beliefs and ritual practices change, and objects lose the value they once had, even though the forms themselves continue to be valued in different ways as works of fine art or transcendent sounds. Social relationships based on age, gender, and hierarchy change, and ethical norms can change in ways that make past practices out of step with present values. Nostalgia for the material and social world of the past is certainly not restricted to any particular society. But it has a different timbre depending on historical circumstances. Loss of language as a result of a deliberate government policy that separates children from their parents and forbids them to speak their own language in schools is very different from speaking a different language than one's parents as a result of migration. Language change is inevitable in a colonial situation and in global and national processes that replace language diversity with lingua francas. But that does not lessen the significance of language loss where it has been used as an instrument of assimilation.

Reconnection with archives and collections can become an integral part of many socio-cultural and identity formation processes. Collections can be the means of uncovering hidden or forgotten histories; recovering and renewing language, song, and techniques of manufacture; retracing genealogical connections; and finding ancestors and images of deceased relatives. The potential is infinite. Hence engagement of source communities requires discovery and the resources to support meaningful connection – access has to be a priority if reengagement is to begin.

Open access and the protocols of connection

Technology today is enabling Indigenous communities to reconnect with objects in museums and make them part of their contemporary lives. Indeed, it is now recognized that many recent collections of Australian Aboriginal material culture were made partly with this purpose in mind, at least as far as the producers were concerned. The opportunity exists for the objects to become part of the ongoing societies of today, no longer viewed as the remains of museum cultures. The ideology of many cultural institutions and researchers has moved towards open access so that the resources of institutions can be of maximum benefit to people and the results of research openly available to all (Pappalardo et al. 2007).

Yet in the case of Indigenous collections, the emphasis has often been placed on the rights of the producing community to control access to objects in museum collections and, in some cases, have the objects returned. While the control of access to and the repatriation of objects are separate issues, they are overlapping. This overlap is signified by the phrase 'digital repatriation', which applies to the return of images, sounds, and information in electronic formats to the producing communities. The process of digital repatriation has resulted in the development of often complex protocols for managing the information once it arrives in the community. Such protocols are also likely to be enforced at the collecting institutions and in the virtual space of the Internet. Many people who support open access in general will support the imposition of protocols that have the potential to radically restrict access to Indigenous collections (see e.g. Hudson and Kenyon 2007). Their arguments may be phrased in terms of differential power relations or the difficulty of getting informed consent.

A culture of protocols is developing in places at the interface between Indigenous cultures and government and cultural institutions. Such protocols give people a degree of agency over museum collections, but it is also important to acknowledge the complexity of the process. For the consequences may otherwise be damaging to the societies themselves and have a negative impact on the ways in which they articulate with the wider world. While well motivated, such sets of protocols can become representations of those cultures to the world and can act as a constraint on the ways in which members of the originating society access material as much as on the access of other museum audiences to the collections. The momentum in the wider world is towards open access. Having too many protocols may constrain the uses that the material can have within the producing society and result in the information contained within museum collections being shut off, just at the moment when broader access is becoming possible. Ironically, at the moment when the potential of the relational museum is being realized, there is a danger that one kind of restriction within museum culture will be replaced by another.

The problems with protocols

Protocols tend to be codifications of behaviour that structure the initial stages of interactions – they may cover correct procedures and processes for making agreements. There is a fine distinction to be made between protocol and etiquette, and between protocols and structures of governance and systems of authority and the power relations associated with them. At one end, protocols can appear innocuous, edging in the direction of good manners, a necessary part of the oil of social interaction, elements in a cultural game, or even an anachronistic heritage from the past. However, they often also attempt to encapsulate core elements of social structures, reflect core values, and incorporate culturally appropriate ways of doing things. Protocols play a crucial role in the domain of diplomacy. Diplomacy often begins with the recognition of different protocols, and, implicitly, those protocols signify cultural difference. Protocols point towards issues of cultural difference and governance that need to be taken into account if agreement is to be reached and if people are going to be able to work together. And in this respect, following protocols is an acknowledgment of people's rights and authority over their own domain.

It is not surprising that protocols have developed as a mechanism for mediating relationships between Indigenous and non-Indigenous peoples, as an integral, if non-juridical, part of the rights agenda. The problems with developing protocols in this context are considerable, even though, on the surface, it seems simply to be due acknowledgement of Indigenous structures of authority and governance. The problems lie in two main areas: the enormous diversity of Indigenous Australian societies and the fact that the acknowledgment of protocols may create an illusion of equality and equivalence between Indigenous and non-Indigenous Australians that in reality is absent. In creating or recognising protocols for engaging with Indigenous Australians, there is a danger of building on a dualistic opposition with non-Indigenous Australians, thus encouraging the idea that one set of protocols will apply equally to all Indigenous Australians. While in many cases the writers of protocols have been scrupulous in trying to avoid the creation of a pan-Aboriginal identity, the very nature of the areas they cover can be taken as a general inventory of difference.

Emergent protocols

Before protocols were written, they were made. A number of general understandings about correct procedures have emerged through interaction between Indigenous and non-Indigenous Australians. While not universally acknowledged, they include the idea that elders held a position of priority in Aboriginal society, that secrecy played a role in creating hierarchies of knowledge, that there was a degree of gender separation into men's business and women's business, and that Aboriginal people had a prior spiritual relationship with their own country. These beliefs – widely held by the non-Aboriginal population, often framed in negative terms – in practice tended to be reinforced in the behaviour of those who viewed Aboriginal society sympathetically. Visitors introduced themselves to the elders first or consulted the elders, secrecy was anticipated, gender separation would be respected, and people would ask whose country they were in. Over time, such practices became formalized, a council of elders might be created, meetings would be divided on the basis of gender, restricted keeping places would be created in museums and communities, and the ceremony of 'welcome to country' evolved. These practices gained authority through articulation with the rights agenda so that they became quite standard ways of respecting Aboriginal authority.

Some elements of protocol, such as welcome to country, have been almost universalized as pan-Aboriginal practice. It is an institution that developed in the late twentieth century, building on the widespread practice of introducing strangers to a country through ceremonial performance. A welcome to country can take many forms and often includes the smoking of the participants using aromatic leaves scorched by fire. In many cases, it has been reduced to a standard formula that is required by an institution before an event can take place. In the absence of Indigenous community representatives, it becomes an 'acknowledgement of the traditional owners of the land'. It would be wrong to see such institutions as being imposed from outside or somehow lacking in authenticity. However, they have the potential to be mere tokens and in other contexts to impose an external framework for enacting Indigenous political processes. They are a product of postcolonial society that have gained in salience because it implicitly acknowledges the prior ownership of the land. As Kristina Everett (2009: 56) writes in the case of the Darug traditional owners of Sydney, the form of the welcome appears

> to be living proof of on-going cultural and linguistic continuity in ways which insist upon Aboriginal presence and identity as 'real'. Darug are able to achieve public recognition successfully using symbolic rituals in ways that are not possible through the legal system.

Written and published protocols have largely developed since the 1970s, although traces of them can be seen in much earlier documents. Initially, protocols developed as documents outlining appropriate ways to work with Aboriginal communities – sometimes they were produced by and for researchers (von Sturmer 1981) and on other occasions for filmmakers (Mackinolty and Duffy 1987). However, recently, more formal documents have been produced. Terri Janke, an Indigenous lawyer and expert in the arts, has been the leading author of a number of them (Mellor and Janke 2001). Such protocols have been careful to emphasize regional variation and the fact that in all cases, the best procedure is to establish a relationship with the local community through appropriate means. Nonetheless, they point towards areas where difference may be found, and there is a danger that they may be interpreted to apply too broadly and too simplistically. For example, two of the rights that need to be respected are the right to 'maintain the secrecy of knowledge and other cultural practices' and 'the right to own and control cultural and intellectual property'. Ownership is subsequently qualified by the statement 'many generations may contribute to the development of an item of knowledge or tradition. In this way, Indigenous cultural heritage is communally owned'.

The problem that writers of protocols face is that, while they need to draw attention to factors that need to be borne in mind and to rights that may apply in a different form to Indigenous than to non-Indigenous Australians, they also need to encompass the diversity and the dynamic nature of Aboriginal societies. Yet they cannot get bogged down in endless qualifications, as they will alienate the very people they are trying to influence.

The digital repatriation of museum collections

Repatriation has been an important component of Australian cultural politics for the last 40 years. The greatest heat has been generated in the area of human remains, as discussed in the previous chapter. Australian museums have been equally responsive to the issue of the repatriation of sacred objects if requested – though clearly this can involve complex definitional issues. Although there have been cases of sacred objects being returned, overall requests for return have been few in number. In a major consultation project undertaken by Museum Victoria, nearly all documented sacred objects had been obtained legitimately by the museum, and the communities asked for the majority to remain in the museum's collection or to be transferred to a regional museum closer to the Indigenous community (Batty 2006).

In the 1980s, there was a movement to create keeping places in a number of communities in remote Australia to which objects from museums could be returned. Although one or two of these have developed into continuing institutions, in particular in the more densely populated areas of south-east Australia, many have fallen into disuse. Such movements need to be seen as stages in an evolving process that is searching for solutions to problems that have only been partially grasped. The idea of local cultural institutions evolving in very different ways in different places according to different regional histories of colonization and contemporary community aspirations is an idea continually in the remaking. In Arnhem Land, relatively few objects have been returned to the communities, and in many cases, the agent for return has been the institution or the individual owner. Unsurprisingly, if objects are to be returned, people might want to return them to life – to make use of them again. On the whole, there has not been a strong demand from the Yolngu for objects to be reincorporated decades after their removal. To an extent, this is because cultural production remains alive; the objects continue to be remade.[1] Old objects are valued, but in many cases, people are happy to use museums as keeping places. And in the present world, museums can give people a strong sense of co-ownership. Indeed, an exceptional case of partial repatriation that proves the rule, the Rirratjingu feather dilly bag gifted to Ronald Berndt by Mawalan Marika that has been brought back to Yirrkala from time to time from the Berndt Museum in Perth for Rirratjingu clan ceremonies. It is removed from its specially constructed travelling box for the performance and then returned to the museum. An additional factor that makes people exercise caution in requesting the return of museum objects is that in many Indigenous communities, art and craft production is a major source of income and community pride. People see present sales of artefacts as being in direct continuity with their forefathers' sale of artefacts to collectors in previous generations and have neither the expectation nor the desire for them to be returned.

In parts of south-east Australia where the gap between colonization and the present is much greater, there is more emphasis on repatriation – though, again, greater curatorial control of and access to collections has been the preferred option. Perhaps the most controversial recent case concerns the bark etchings collected by the squatter John Hunter Kerr from the Kulin people of Victoria in 1854. The objects were originally collected for the Sandhurst Exhibition held that year in Bendigo. Eventually, after a tour of a number of international exhibitions overseas, three bark etchings ended up first at Royal Botanic Gardens, Kew, and then in 1866, two were given to the British Museum. In 2004, the objects were loaned back by the British Museum to become the core of an exhibition eponymously titled 'Etched on Bark 1854'. At the end of the exhibition, Gary Murray a leader of the Dja Dja Wurrung people, claimed the objects for repatriation and took out an injunction under Subsection 21C of the Commonwealth Government's Aboriginal and Torres Strait Islander Heritage Protection Act 1984 that initially prevented their return to the United Kingdom. The case was eventually lost, and the objects were returned to the British Museum. Elizabeth Willis, the curator who organized the exhibition, has written an insightful analysis of the events (Willis 2008). She details how in the staging of the exhibition great attention was paid to existing protocols. The regional Indigenous group was fully involved in the exhibition and its opening. She explains the subsequent request for return partly in terms of the particular moment in time at which it occurred: the Yorta Yorta people had lost their native title claim and felt deeply aggrieved by what they saw as the failure of legal process. However, she also shows how the Australian media seized on the case as an example of the iniquities of British colonialism and the tainted nature of museum collections. The headline in the national newspaper *The Age* was 'Taking Aim at Hunter-Gather England'.[2] Ultimately, Willis argues that there was a positive outcome in the community's reengagement with objects that had previously been lost to memory. This resulted in etching on burnt bark returning as an artistic practice in the present generation.

Although there has not been a strong demand for the repatriation of actual objects in recent years, there has been a strong demand for the digital repatriation of images. While this may at first seem to be a contradiction, an analysis of the context quickly makes it clear why it is not. Indigenous Australians, as much as anyone, are moving into an age of digital imagery, and digital images have multiple uses. They can be stored readily in large numbers and reproduced when required. Their uses range from cultural education in schools, developing displays in art centres, and researching family and community histories. In many areas, the most sought-after images are photographs of people from the past.

A digital repatriation case study: Yirrkala

In Yirrkala, there is a history of valuing photographs – people have always held one or two images of relatives, ceremonies, or paintings among their dearest possessions. Until recently, photographs have had relatively short lifetimes – held and passed around until they disintegrate. However, Yolngu are quick to seize on the potential of technology to prolong the life of images, and as soon as the facility became available, people would take photographs to be laminated at the pharmacy in the local mining town or the community education centre. Although the lifetime of actual photographs remained short, people often knew who had taken them and would request further copies. Photographs are memories of people. The Yolngu seek out photographs taken by the founding missionaries and the first anthropologists in order to identify their relatives from the past and connect them to the present. Today, at every funeral, the Yolngu research and request photographs of the deceased at different stages of his or her life and decorate the shade where the body lies or the vehicle that takes the coffin to the graveyard with photographs of the dead person and their ancestors.[3] Non-Indigenous visitors often find this disturbing because it contradicts one of the fundamental presuppositions about Aboriginal culture held by outsiders – that upon death, all direct forms of reference to the dead person, in particular images and names, are repressed. This viewpoint is reinforced in every film or documentary on Indigenous Australia by the warning message that 'this film may contain images of deceased people.' There is no question that such messages are well motivated if sometimes ill worded – nonetheless, a consequence is the othering of the Indigenous population as a category in a way that belies the complexity of Indigenous responses to and uses of images. It also fails to track the dynamism of Aboriginal society and the fact that communities tend to be active in managing changed circumstances. The educational role of protocols has to be balanced against their generalizing tendencies.

In the last decade, the repatriation of images has been facilitated by digital technology. Initially, access to images came through schools and art centres. However, in many communities, this has been formalized either through the creation of Indigenous knowledge and cultural centres or by an extension of library services. Buku Larrnggay Mulka, the art centre at Yirrkala, for example, has created a separate knowledge centre within the organization. The knowledge centre is well equipped with computer terminals and is developing its own database of images by acquiring collections from cultural institutions and collections of photographs and films from missionaries and anthropologists. The knowledge centre aims both to provide services for the Yolngu and to present Yolngu culture to the outside world. It is managed by a Yolngu board and mainly staffed by Yolngu. As well as being a centre for distribution, it is increasingly becoming a centre for contemporary image production, with Yolngu staff recording community events, including ceremonial performances. The centre also contains a collection of paintings and objects that are used primarily as an attraction for tourists but which undoubtedly provide a future asset for the community. The central piece is a work of great value to the Yolngu themselves – the Church Panels that are held in a special side 'chapel' set off from the main building. As Christen (2007: 102) argues with reference to the Warumungu Nyinkka Nyunyu cultural centre at Tennant Creek, such centres leverage 'the *possibility* of connecting economic sustainability with culturally viable local projects'.

There have been a number of research projects working with the knowledge centre that have involved the repatriation of images and information from museum and private collections. Clearly, it is easier to obtain images from cultural institutions than private collections. The former is better known, and the institutions are usually willing to take part in the process.

On the other hand, collections made in the past by anthropologists, missionaries, and others have often been dispersed across a number of institutions, and over time, knowledge of their location is often lost. Very occasionally, the collection remains as a whole in one place. Donald Thomson's collection from eastern Arnhem Land, made over the period from 1935 to 1943, remains in its entirety (on loan from the University of Melbourne) at Melbourne Museum (Allen 2008). However, more usually, the opposite is the case. The collections of the pioneer anthropologist of the Yolngu, Lloyd Warner, made in the 1920s at Milingimbi shortly after the establishment of the first mission station in the area, is divided between at least ten institutions in Australia and America. And because of the nature of Western archival practices and Western knowledge systems, the collection has been divided on the basis of artefact type. Films and photographs have been stored in one institution or part of an institution, objects in another, and print material and documents in another. Thus a primary task that the Yolngu face before material can be returned is to find out where it has been distributed. An alliance has developed between the Yolngu, researchers, and cultural institutions both to search for the material and to facilitate its return. The main task, apart from digitizing the imagery itself, is the development of search engines and databases to enable access to materials. This is where the issue of protocols enters the picture.

The easiest way to repatriate images is through open access collection databases. Once an object is located, high-resolution images can be requested. Many public institutions are oriented towards distributing images in this way as a service to the community. Such processes crosscut the boundary between public and private knowledge, enabling anyone to view private family photographs from the past if they are archived in public institutions. This is something that needs to be managed sensitively, but on the whole, in a Western context, this has not developed as a major issue. Indeed, the problematic areas are more likely to concern matters of copyright and control, which may inhibit the dissemination of images (see Hudson and Kenyon 2007). However, it is not hard to imagine images that would offend people if they were widely distributed on the Internet or available to all members of a particular community – images of dying people, victims of crimes of violence or war, photographs of private moments. Cross-culturally, that can be seen to be a major issue. Cultural sensitivity varies enormously, and the possibility of offence is considerable. Quite rightly, these factors emerged early on in discussions of the repatriation of photographs and collections to Indigenous communities (see Christen 2009). And this is an area where the protocols of diplomacy and the protocols of the digital age come together in the discourse of access and rights in images.

In the digital world, protocols are the procedures and sets of rules required to allow access to images digitally – to communicate between computers and to access databases. It is necessary initially to distinguish between two issues – global access to cultural materials that are housed in museum collections and access to data by members of the community of origin. These two are related since anything that is on open access globally is likely to be accessible locally unless it is specifically blocked. The most effective way to block global distribution is to do so at the source of the image by requesting the holding institution to remove it from web access. The issue I am focussing on in this chapter is the control of local access. However, in many cases, the same databases and often the same interfaces serve a dual purpose (see e.g. Christen 2009).

Protocols can become part of the world of the imaginary, and in the case of Aboriginal society, they can involve, in effect, the creation of models of the operation of Aboriginal society, which are then used to regulate the distribution of information. When discussing these matters with information technology specialists, everything becomes possible. We can create systems of access with different orders of passwords that will enable members of a community to access centrally held information differentially on the basis of age, gender, and group affiliation. But although that is possible, deciding on who actually has the right to access the information is a quite different order of problem. Anthropologically, we know how difficult it is to model social structure, and applying such models to the management of information is likely to be highly problematic. There is the danger of reifying a particular state of a dynamic system, freezing it in time, and forcing people to act as if it was the permanent unchanging real world. People can be literally locked out of access to knowledge on that basis. And we have not yet begun to consider what the boundaries are of the community of users. Who decides who can use the system and who decides what images should be constrained by the system?

In terms of moral rights, the idea of restricting access has considerable force, and it does engage with important issues of respect for cultural difference and control of cultural production. Hence considerable energy has been devoted to the development of databases and search engines that enable access to be restricted on the basis of a considerable range of criteria. Indeed, major government-funded projects have been prefaced by the requirement to establish methods of repatriation that are sensitive to the social structures of the communities concerned. In one case, a government-funded project to implement the repatriation of images lasted for three years, and in the end, not a single image was repatriated – the project remained at the phase of establishing agreed protocols for return. This signals the difficulty and is the product of the fact that Indigenous communities are extremely diverse.

It is, and will continue to be, very difficult to develop models that apply on an Australia-wide basis.

A number of projects developed with Indigenous communities have created culturally sensitive means of access. The best known in Australia is the Ara Irititja database, developed initially for communities in the Aṉangu Pitjantjatjara Yankunytjatjara Lands of central Australia where restrictions on the basis of gender are stronger than elsewhere in Australia. The system was originally developed for the digital repatriation of photographs from mission archives. It is capable of being adapted to the requirements of different communities and has been used by the North Territory Libraries Board in communities across northern Australia. The problem with such a system is that it needs to be continually updateable in the local context, both according to contingent events and to changing circumstances – it may be necessary to remove images of the recently deceased or to open access as the climate of opinion changes. Though clearly in the real world, people will be able to find their way around constraints by sharing codes or viewing images collectively.

And here is the nub of my argument: should systems of regulated access be built into the systems for returning data to communities, should they be part of the process of digital repatriation at all stages, or should the local community be allowed to institute its own controls locally in the operation of an a priori open access system? The advantage of the latter is clearly that it enables the much more rapid digital repatriation of material. The fear that those who advocate control have is that the wrong image shown to the wrong person at the wrong time may have negative consequences. A woman seeing her dead brother may cut her head in mourning and break down inconsolably; a woman seeing a photograph of a secret phase of an initiation ceremony may be beaten or driven from the community. Certainly, the viewing of such images is likely to cause trauma in some cases. However, both of these examples contain complexities. Displays of grief are a normal part of life in many societies and are triggered by many different factors – the mention of a name, the singing of a song, the sight of a photograph, the visit of a relative. Controlling the mourning process is built into the Yolngu social process; grief is anticipated and responded to (Morphy and Morphy 2012). To outsiders, it seems out of control; from within, it is a normal part of life. In the past, images of the dead were a major trigger for displays of grief, but as images have become part of the everyday, their impact has been reduced, and, as we have seen, they are now introduced into the funeral ceremony itself. It clearly is going to be necessary to restrict some images, in particular of secret phases of ceremonies, by removing them where possible from publicly accessible databases – this applies both to community-developed databases and to information available via the Internet.

My position on this is biased by my own experience of working with the Yolngu to try to develop a search engine that could harvest data from museum collections around the world and make it accessible to community members. Aware of the discourse over controlling access, I had anticipated that this might be a significant issue. However, I was also aware that the Yolngu managed the circulation of images within their own society just as they manage access to restricted contexts and places. I discussed three topics with Yolngu managers of the knowledge centre: access on the basis of clan, access to restricted images, and need to restrict images of the dead. In all cases, the answers that came back were both pragmatic and to an extent anticipated. As far as clan-specific images were concerned, it was argued that since clans intermarry and each person's network of kin is unique but overlaps with that of others, restriction on the basis of clan was inappropriate. However, searching on the basis of clan was quite a different matter – that was how people would begin to search for images. In other words, where possible, clan association should be coded as metadata. As to the danger of accessing restricted images, the question was immediately thrown back to me: 'Who will know that the images are restricted? We will, and then we can make a decision'. 'But what if someone accesses them who shouldn't?' 'We will tell them not to'. The view was very strongly expressed that the Yolngu wanted maximum access to material as expeditiously as possible, and that when they had the material, they would be able to manage it. And on the issue of photographs of the deceased, the discussion again was very revealing. We suggested developing a system that would enable images of recently dead people to be removed. The response was that it would be better if rather than being removed absolutely the image was masked and an option provided that could allow a person to open an image if they wished to. It was also suggested that a time limit would be imposed on the masking so that the image would be opened again after six months. If necessary, the closure could be reimposed. These suggestions clearly reflect both Yolngu knowledge of their own practices and acknowledged individual differences and change over time.

People will be affected by images of the recent dead in very different ways. Death is precisely the time when certain relatives will be set the task of finding images of the dead person. Yet at the same time, other people need to be protected from the grief triggered by the image of a close relative. Warning people that an image may contain sensitive information gives them a choice. The desire to keep the images on the system and to impose a limit on the length of time they are closed reveals a sophisticated understanding of administrative systems. The chances are if something is removed, it will be a long time before it is put back again. However, the time limit also reflects the subtlety of Yolngu practice. In the case of a good death, the death from natural causes of an elderly person, images and names quickly become less painful, whereas in the case of traumatic and untimely deaths, there may be a need to impose the bar for many years to come.

The consultation with Yolngu at the Buku Larrnggay Mulka centre demonstrated both a pragmatic and a culturally informed response to the issue of local protocols. Digitization was seen as a technology that afforded significant opportunities, and the emphasis was directed away from protocols towards facilitation. Indeed, when researchers discussed the question of accessing the database, Yolngu consultants expressed a desire not to have individual passwords (or passwords at all for that matter) and to 'control access ourselves'. Hence the system that was developed required a single community password entered once and could be saved on the computer.

Yolngu communities compared

In some other Yolngu communities, initial stages of repatriation have included modelling the development of databases with complex protocols of access. An excellent study has been carried out by Jessica DeLargy Healy on the development of a database associated with a knowledge centre at the neighbouring Yolngu community of Galiwin'ku. In this case, she shows how, as part of the exercise of developing the knowledge centre, community members did attempt to develop a system of access that modelled structural features of their society. The model produced was impressive as a representation for condensing and communicating the key structural dynamics of the Yolngu world.[4] However, she also shows how in many respects, what was developed as model proved unworkable in practice – but this did not inhibit the community getting on with the task of digital repatriation. What worked well was Yolngu engagement with the museum communities, which resulted in a process of repatriation that reintroduced the material back into to the flow of Yolngu life. The emphasis was, as in the Yirrkala case, on enabling the objects to return and then bringing them under the control of local protocols. Interestingly, this is very much in harmony with the conclusion that Nakata et al. (2008: 25) come to when reviewing the issues involved in the digitization of Indigenous collections: 'Without a shadow of doubt, the Indigenous preference would be to begin at a different primary point [than legal and sensitivity issues] viz. the need for Indigenous access to Indigenous materials in collections'.

In the case of both the Yirrkala and Galiwin'ku communities, there is a strong sense that the problem of controlling access to returned material is no different than the general process of controlling knowledge within the society. Each community is well organized and confident that it can control the distribution of knowledge within its community as it always has done.

Knowledge is controlled by people and by the awareness and respect that people have of the boundaries and principles of access that they have as individuals. Yolngu society is one in which nearly everything can be seen or heard by those who choose to look and listen but in which people reveal through use and performance only that which they are publicly acknowledged to know and have the right and authority to use.

The fact that the Yolngu seem to place little stress on conditions of access when discussing digital repatriation does not mean that they are not concerned with their cultural rights or with the difference between Yolngu knowledge systems and teaching practice and those of the encapsulating society. Rather, they see digital repatriation as a mechanism that can be used to their advantage. Certainly, the Yolngu engage with the idea of developing culturally appropriate databases and are aware of the need to represent their system of knowledge in relation to their own local epistemologies and systems of value. They do this from a distinctly relativistic perspective, which allows for difference. The Yolngu have pioneered what is referred to as 'two-way learning' in which their children learn both according to Yolngu and European epistemologies while keeping them relatively separate. The emphasis is on learning both ways and seeing the relationship between different ways of knowing the world. Two-way learning was formalized as a practical Yolngu initiative to include their system of knowledge within the school curriculum as a parallel mode of education to the Western curriculum (Marika-Mununggiritj 1999). The inclusion of Yolngu knowledge within the constraints of the school system involved changes to the ways in which such knowledge is passed on by codifying and reproducing it in the form of books and packaged teaching materials. It also introduced a new context of transmission. Whereas outside-of-school clan membership and gender are factors that structure the transmission of knowledge, the school classroom is a mixed gender, multiclan environment. In including Yolngu knowledge in the school curriculum, the Yolngu were required to make choices that they might not otherwise have made, but they did so as conscious agents, weighing the advantages against the disadvantages. Their argument for two-way education is that if Yolngu knowledge is left outside the school system, then Western knowledge systems will be privileged. The inclusion of Yolngu knowledge as a separate component within the school curriculum presupposes its difference yet simultaneously asserts its equivalence.

This reflection opens up what might be seen as the reciprocal issue to enabling local access: that is controlling access by non-Yolngu to material held in institutions outside Yolngu society. Historically, the emphasis that Yolngu have adopted has been to share knowledge while maintaining control. The Yolngu have extended the boundaries of their system of knowledge to include the encapsulating society that surrounds them – bringing them in so that they understand the Yolngu part of 'two-way learning'. They wish to engage with the outside world, and they see the collections of their material culture, the recordings of their music, and the ritual performances as part of this process. They institute control primarily not by denying access and closing themselves off from the outside world but by actively engaging with it. This does not mean that everything will be open access. The Yolngu, in effect, maintain restrictions within their own society by broadening those restrictions to include members of the encapsulating society.

Conclusion

Since intensive European colonization began in the 1920s and '30s, the Yolngu have consciously used art, material culture, and performance as a means of engaging with the colonial Australian society for economic return, as a means of persuading people of the value of their way of life, and in defence of their rights. The process resulted in the creation of major distributed archives and collections of Yolngu cultural production in museums in Australia and overseas. In recent years, the Yolngu have been closely involved in co-curating a number of exhibitions in major museums and galleries (see e.g. Morphy 2006). Yolngu participation in such projects often shows a deep understanding of the potential for collaboration with external institutions to achieve a number of different objectives. Banduk Marika conceived of a number of related projects to ensure that her clan country of Yalangbara received recognition and protection for its environmental and cultural significance. Her initial aim was to gain recognition for the place on the register of the national estate as an inspirational landscape. She researched collections in museums and art galleries around Australia to gather supporting material for the application. She succeeded in this initial objective and then saw the potential to use the material in producing a book (West 2008) and an exhibition that gave recognition to the artistic heritage that stems from Yalangbara.

Yolngu retain restricted contexts and restricted bodies of knowledge. But in general, most Yolngu knowledge is open to all members of Yolngu society, and that public knowledge in different ways has been opened up to the world outside. In the rare case of material that has been inappropriately released outside in the past, the Yolngu look to the holding institutions themselves to participate in the process of controlling access. On rare occasions, material has been returned but more generally the Yolngu have been involved instead in the way those materials have been curated within the institutions. This has meant that the Yolngu, rather than emphasizing protocols for restricting knowledge, have been more oriented towards spreading knowledge and understanding. It also places Yolngu control of their own society's knowledge as something that the Yolngu share in common with Australian society more generally. Restricted access and privacy are part of the life of all societies and seen in that light can help maintain autonomy yet at the same time close distance.

Protocols are historically the basis of making agreements and sharing understandings. While getting outsiders to understand that some areas of Yolngu society are restricted in access, the protocols devised by the Yolngu are oriented towards opening up to others those areas that are not. The Yolngu are also happy to develop partnerships over restrictions of access with European institutions, availing themselves of the safe storage facilities provided by museums and getting the museums to ensure the privacy of some of the contents. The emphasis thus has been not on restriction but on opening up almost to the point of conversion.[5] Participation in national and global discourse may be a better way of correcting misunderstandings than shutting the world away.

Notes

1 Barbara Glowczewsk (2016: 160) reports a similar attitude in Paris in 1983 when Warlbiri dancers from Central Australia performing at the Festival d'Automne were shown sacred objects housed in a museum's collection. She notes, 'Following the example of a recent museographic movement, the curator proposed a restitution . . . an elder concluded "We have the same sacred objects that we still use today. The French can keep the ones they have in exchange for the way they have welcomed us" '.

2 *The Age*, 31 July 2004. www.theage.com.au/articles/2004/07/30/1091080431749.html (Accessed 2 June 2013).

3 In Yirrkala, when we began fieldwork in the early 1970s, people exercised extreme caution in exposing people to images of the recently dead. Over time, attitudes have changed and photographs of the recently dead have become desired objects, as Deger (2008) confirms is the case in the neighboring Yolngu community of Gapuwiyak. However, photographs are still treated as objects whose power has to be controlled, and the taboo on uttering the names of the deceased and associated homophones remains strong.

4 A similar exercise was carried out by Kimberly Christen working with community members to develop a web resource that is structured according to the access protocols of the Warumungu community of Tennant Creek. The site allows access according to Warumungu 'modes of information sharing based on the cultural protocols that define how, when and by whom information should be viewed and with a place, a video clip may stop halfway through because the material is restricted by gender, or audio of a song may fade in and out because elements are restricted to only those who have been ritually initiated, or a photo may be only half visible because someone in the photo has died'.

5 See e.g. Morphy (2005, 2006).

References

Allen, L. (2008) "Tons and tons of valuable material: the Donald Thomson collection," in Peterson, N., Allen, L. and Hamby, L. (eds) *The Makers and Making of Indigenous Australian Museum Collections*, pp. 392–424, Melbourne: Melbourne University Press.

Batty, P. (2006) "White redemption rituals: reflections on the repatriation of Aboriginal secret-sacred objects," in Lea, T., Kowal, E. and Cowlishaw, G. (eds) *Moving Anthropology: Critical Indigenous Studies*, pp. 55–65, Darwin: Charles Darwin University Press.

Christen, K. (2007) "Following the Nyinkka: relations of respect and obligations to act in the collaborative work of Aboriginal Cultural Centers," *Museum Anthropology*, 30 (2): 101–124.

Christen, K. (2009) "Access and accountability: the ecology of information sharing in the digital age," *Anthropology News*, 'Visual Ethics', April: 4–5.

Deger, J. (2008) "Imprinting on the heart: photography and contemporary Yolngu mournings," *Visual Anthropology*, 21: 292–309.

Everett, K. (2009) "Welcome to country . . . not," *Oceania*, 79 (1): 53–64.

Glowczewsk, B. (2016) *Desert Dreamers*, Minneapolis: University of Minnesota Press and Univocal Publishing.

Hudson, E. and Kenyon, A. (2007) "Without walls: copyright law and digital collections in Australian cultural institutions," *SCRIPT-ed*, 4 (2): 197–213.

Mackinolty, C. and Duffy, M. (1987) *Guess Who's Coming to Dinner in Arnhem Land*, Darwin: Research and Communications Branch, Northern Land Council.

Marika-Mununggiritj, R. (1999) "The 1998 Wentworth lecture," *Australian Aboriginal Studies*, 1: 3–9.

Mellor, D. and Janke, T. (2001) *Valuing Art, Respecting Culture: Protocols for Working with the Australian Indigenous Visual Arts and Craft Sector*, Sydney: National Association for the Visual Arts.

Morphy, F. and Morphy, H. (2012) "Soon we will be spending all our time at funerals," in Howe, S. and Talle, A. (eds) *Returns to the Field*, pp. 49–72, Bloomington: Indiana University Press.

Morphy, H. (2005) "Mutual conversion? The Methodist Church and the Yolngu, with particular reference to Yirrkala," *Humanities Research*, 12 (1): 41–53.

Morphy, H. (2006) "Sites of persuasion: Yingapungapu at National Museum of Australia," in Karp, I., Kratz, C., Swatja, L. and Ybarra-Frausto, T. (eds) *Museum Frictions: Public Cultures/Global Transformations*, pp. 469–496, Durham, NC: Duke University Press.

Nakata, M., McKeough, J., Gardiner, G., Byrne, A., Gibson, J. and Nakata, V. (2008) *Australian Indigenous Collections: First Generation Issues*, Broadway: University of Technology Sydney and UTSeScholarship.

Pappalardo, K.M., Fitzgerald, A.M., Fitzgerald, B.F. and Kiel-Chisholm, S.D. (2007) *A Guide to Open Access Through Your Digital Repository*, Brisbane: Queensland University of Technology.

von Sturmer, J. (1981) "Talking with aborigines," *Australian Institute of Aboriginal Studies Newsletter*, 15: 13–20.

West, M. (ed) (2008) *Yalangbara: Art of the Djang'kawu*, Darwin: Charles Darwin University Press.

Willis, E. (2008) "The law, politics, and 'historical wounds': the Dja Dja Wurrung bark etchings case in Australia," *International Journal of Cultural Property*, 15 (1): 49–63.

6 Conclusion

Collections, time, and identity

My end and my beginning return to a line from James Fenton's poetic reflections on the Pitt Rivers Museum.

> *We cannot either feel that we have come*
> *Far or in any particular direction.*

Poetry has the capacity to bring ideas and experiences to the front of the mind and let them roam. I could go in many directions. But first and foremost, Fenton captured the wonder I felt as a child visitor, and later as a privileged curator of the museum, of the richness of human creativity and imagination. As a child, I sensed that although the objects came from many different places and times, they were all produced by people like me and should not be framed as signs of progress but appreciated in their own right. Yet at the same time, Fenton's words come out of a value-creation process, with its origins in the Enlightenment, in which attitudes to human diversity changed over time. The idea that we have not come 'far or in any particular direction' is very different from the evolutionism of General Pitt Rivers who built the collection. The change in perception requires a form of relativism that places objects in their own cultural and historical contexts rather than ranking them in evolutionary sequences.

The passionate engagement of many of the builders of ethnographic collections reflected a positive wonder at difference. In a local context, the collections are frequently the product of collaborative processes, but the objects often become separated from those processes over time. Such is the nature of building collections to last and to become part of new and often fundamentally different collaborative processes. So in seeing that we have not come in any particular direction and that difference is not meaningfully ranked in terms of linear progression, there has been some movement. And further movement, to be productive, cannot be a denial of change nor can it neglect the role of technological innovation in the trajectories of human societies. Rather, it is not to make singular factors primary criteria for valuing human societies.

***

This book has two core themes: value-creation processes associated with museum collections and the spatio-temporal disjunctions that material objects both evoke and allow people to transcend. Both of these are viewed from a position of globalization in which differences and inequalities are being made on a scale and rate that differs from the past. The history of museums cannot be separated from the history of European colonization, but museums are also connected to an equally important though relatively autonomous trajectory of globalization. Both historical processes have to be seen as trajectories of change in which the world has been transformed and values have changed dramatically over time.

I have argued that museum collections are deeply entangled in value-creation processes and that indeed the use of and attitude towards museum collections is at times both in step and out of step with such processes. The outcome of research, collection and exhibition is to change the value of things in the present and to add to our understanding of the past. Changing how things are valued depends on the context and regime of value in which they are placed. Collections and archives provide a resource for understanding how the objects were valued at the time of collection, both by the source communities and by the collectors. The value-creation processes often change their meaning and significance – they almost become different objects, yet they do not leave their past behind. Indeed, the ideology of the museum – its best practice – is that the past is carried forward with the object. The museum should retain the old labels; the catalogue entries should be added to, not overwritten; the exhibitions and loans should be recorded. Infinity is glimpsed through change.

Time is a difficult concept to grasp, and anthropological discourse about time has engaged with its complexities in analyzing trajectories of technological change, seasonal cycles, systems of exchange, kinship and bestowal, and even thinking reflexively about how anthropology may or may not position people in relation to past, present, and future. Time is of particular relevance in understanding and engaging with collections in museums and archives.[1] In researching the past, in engaging the past, it is important to understand that we are entering another time, not through a linear timeline in which the world is somehow moving in a coordinated way, but through a time that is a conjunction of different pasts and presents and different trajectories. The perspective from infinity, or at least the *longue durée*, means that museum objects are of the present and yet in another sense have no place or time of their own. The distinction I make between the source community and the museum community is centred on two of the trajectories in which the same object can be placed, but both have histories of discontinuity and displacement.

I will illustrate this point with two objects from Australia that could have been made at the same time by Indigenous people inhabiting the same continent but which in many respects belong to very different and relatively autonomous space-times. They were both selected for exhibitions of the British Museum collections that I was involved in. We met them briefly in earlier chapters.

Container and spear

They are the kelp water carrier from Tasmania that was made around 1850 and the ceremonial spear (*baṯi*) from eastern Arnhem Land in the 1870s. Both objects were of a kind that could have been made centuries, perhaps millennia, before the date of their collection. The kelp container was made at Oyster Cove in Tasmania, where Indigenous Tasmanians (Palawa) had been in effect held in custody but continued to gain sustenance from the resources of the land, perform their songs and ceremonies, and make objects for themselves and to sell to outsiders. The kelp container (Figure 6.1) in the British Museum collection is the only one to survive from this time.

The Yolngu spear (Figure 6.2) was made by people who were still living beyond the colonial frontier as it moved across Australia from south to north. The Yolngu engaged in trade with people from Makassar, visited the islands of Indonesia, and exchanged names. Yolngu and Macassarese performed in each other's ceremonies. The Yolngu too made artefacts for home consumption and for trade. Yolngu land had already been notionally incorporated under the sovereignty of the British Crown, but the Yolngu at existed in a very different space-time than the Indigenous people of Tasmania. From a Euro-Australian perspective, they were the other side of the frontier. Their loss of sovereignty under British and Australian law only begun to have a major local impact in the twentieth century. In 1907, the trade with the Makassans came to an abrupt end when the traders were forced to pay taxes. As the twentieth century moved on, they had to struggle increasingly against incursions into their land. But in the middle of the nineteenth century, Palawa and Yolngu lived in different spatio-temporal zones.

The history of the two objects in the museum, their history of exhibition, and their contemporary significance to source communities reflect the different yet overlapping positions they occupied in the mid-nineteenth

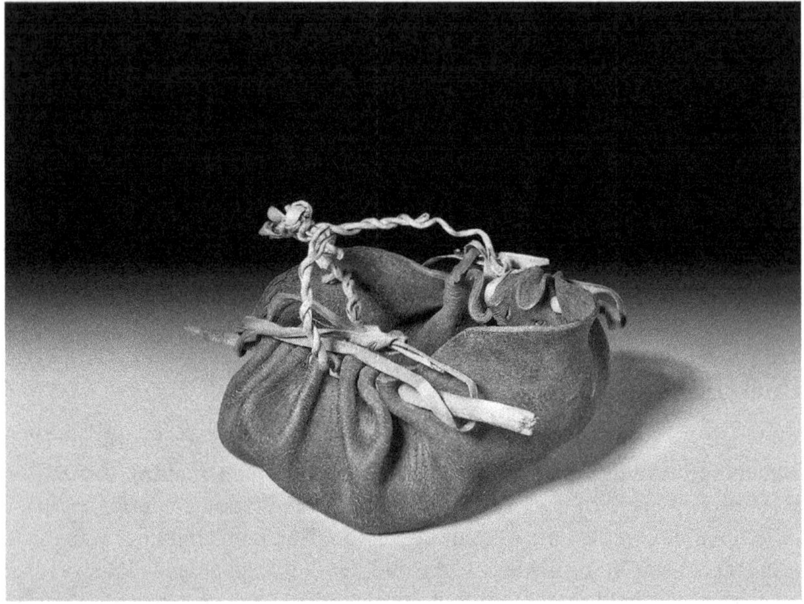

Figure 6.1 Kelp water container, probably from, c. 1851, Oyster Cove, Tasmania. British Museum, London. Reproduced with permission.

Credit: British Museum

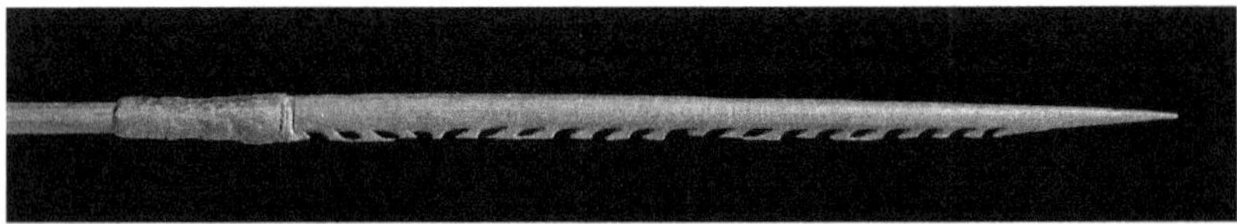

Figure 6.2 Baṯi, Eastern Arnhem Land, Northern Territory of Australia, before 1879. British Museum, London. Reproduced with permission.

Credit: British Museum

century. Differences in the past have consequences both on the value of the objects to descendants of the original makers and the value that they have as museum objects. The Tasmanian kelp basket in the British Museum's collection was first exhibited in the Great Exhibition of 1851 to exemplify the use of kelp as a raw material for manufacture. In the British Museum in the nineteenth century, it would have been seen as a functional object made by a person from a hunter-gather society. It was originally labelled as a pitcher referring to its function as a water container and fitted into the more general categories of baskets and containers. Small in size and exquisite in appearance, it was labelled as a possible model. Placed in a nineteenth-century evolutionary framework of hunter-gather society, it could have been used to represent earlier stages in the technological and social complexity of human societies, though there is no evidence that it actually was. Over the past 50 years, its growing significance has arguably been reflected in its inclusion in a series of exhibitions that brought the British Museum's Indigenous Australian collections to the public. It was first exhibited in 1972 as part of *The Australian Aborigines*, which was one of the opening exhibitions of the short-lived Museum of Mankind.[2] In 2011, after the Department of Ethnography had been relocated back to the main building, the basket was exhibited in *Baskets and Belonging: Indigenous Australian Histories*. In 2015, it took its place in the temporary exhibition *Indigenous Australia: Enduring Civilisation*, which was followed in 2016 in a move back to Australia for a reciprocal exhibition, *Encounters*, in the National Museum of Australia.

The Yolngu *baṯi* from Arnhem Land had a very different history in the museum's collection. It was collected in Sulawesi in 1879 by the Norwegian diplomat, collector, and naturalist Carl Alfred Bock. On a short stopover in Pale Pale, Bock asked the Raja to assist him in acquiring a collection from the region. The spear was one of the objects acquired. Clearly not from Sulawesi, it resided in the British Museum collections misidentified as a spear from New Guinea until the 1950s. It was recognized by the anthropologist Charles Mountford in 1956 as coming from Arnhem Land.[3]

The miscataloguing is interesting for many reasons. Bock was in most cases a systematic collector who spent time in the communities he visited, documenting the collections he made. Pale Pale was an opportunistic visit. The boat he was travelling on stopped there briefly, and in his account of the visit, he records that he had to leave in a hurry when he heard ships siren sound for departure. He would have been aware that Sulawesi was a centre of regional trade and recognized that the spears were not local. But in the 1870s, the European colonization of northern Australia was in its early stages. Eastern Arnhem Land was beyond the colonial frontier; no material culture from the region existed in European collections. In the European imagination, Australia was still a land that had been cut off from the rest of the world – *Terra Australis Incognita*. Unlike the kelp basket from Tasmania, the Yolngu *baṯi* was arguably an unknown object from an uncontacted society. Indeed, the realization that Indigenous Australians, far from being isolated from the rest of the world, were very much part of regional systems of trade and exchange networks would itself challenge European preconceptions about Aboriginal societies.

There is no record of the *baṯi* being exhibited in the British Museum prior to *Enduring Civilisation* and *Encounters*.

The history of the kelp water carrier and the *baṯi* illustrate the value-creation processes associated with museums and ethnographic collections and their entanglement with European history. Over time, the water carrier has become a symbol of the devastating consequences of the colonization of Tasmania by the British. Its uniqueness tells its own story and in recent exhibitions, that story has come to the fore. However, value operates in many dimensions. The inclusion of the kelp vessel in an exhibition called *Baskets and Belonging: Indigenous Australian Histories* reflects a major change that has occurred over time both in the recognition of value in material objects made by women and in challenging the neglect of craft as creative practice. Indeed, as I have argued elsewhere, the growing appreciation of Indigenous material culture – its aesthetic forms and technical accomplishment – has played an active role in changing Western categories (Morphy 2007). At the same time, in the title of the exhibition, the emotional dimension of material objects and the link to place are signalled.

Two exhibitions

The linked exhibitions *Enduring Civilisation* and *Encounters* each had different themes that gave the objects included in the two exhibitions a different resonance.[4] *Enduring Civilisation* was aimed at a British audience to show the richness of the British Museum's Australian collections and to emphasize the central place of Indigenous Australians in contemporary Australia and their significant place in world history. Making people conscious of the consequences of colonization, the exhibition made no attempt to hide the uncomfortable history of some of the objects nor to mask their contested nature. The exhibition also had Australian audiences in mind, both Indigenous and non-Indigenous. International exhibitions are one of the ways in which objects and ideas gain global currency, and this can have a significant impact on home communities and audiences. Indigenous involvement in the exhibition was strong, and the works were included after extensive community consultation. It was clearly significant that the lead curator of the exhibition Dr Gaye Sculthorpe, head of the Oceanic section at the British Museum, is an Indigenous Tasmanian.

Some objects in the exhibition collected by Constable Ord on punitive expeditions through Bunuba country in the Kimberley in the 1890s were among the most uncomfortable. Bunuba leader June Oscar's response when she visited the exhibition in London was consistent with the curators objectives

The British Museum's "enduring civilization" is a powerful step towards honouring our living history. In her public lecture given at the time of the opening, she said,

> Both older and present day objects draw attention to the unsettled and emergent dialogue that is ever unfolding between our Indigenous nation's claims to self-determination and sovereignty, which we have never relinquished, and the Australian nation-state's imposed governmental and legislative authority over the entire continent.
>
> It is our triumph that in the heart of London, with the seat of government that once upon a time threatened to demolish us just down the road, that our lives and heritages have come to be displayed through our equal consent and involvement.
>
> (Oscar 2015: 26–27)

The *Encounters* exhibition held the following year at the National Museum of Australia in Canberra, and curated independently, included many of the objects that had been in the British Museum exhibition. The theme of continuity remained central, as was engagement with source communities. During the consultation period that had taken place over the previous four years, objects had been commissioned to juxtapose with those from the British Museum's collection. Some of the objects reflected continuities from the very beginnings of European colonization. The pronged fish spears (*garrara*) illustrated in drawings from the First Fleet and collected on Cook's voyage continue to be made by descendants from the region. One made by Gweagal man Rod Mason was included in the exhibition. Other objects were from innovative traditions that had developed post-colonization, such as the 'Sydney Harbour Bridge' shell ornament made by Esme Timbery.

The exhibition included commentaries from the different communities, some in the form of text panels and others as filmed statements that addressed the visitors directly and had a powerful impact. Indigenous Tasmanians have in recent years worked closely with museum collections and archival records and created continuities of practice with past technologies and aesthetic practices. This was the focus of Tessa Atto's commentary:

> I think a main point would be not to focus so much on the invasion and colonization . . . [but] to look back at what we had beforehand, which we still have today, like the making [of] shell necklaces, and the bracelets, making baskets, working with *ricau*, which is the bull kelp. I think those things happened forever and are still happening today.
>
> (Atto 2015: 207)

A complementary exhibition in an adjacent gallery exhibited a series of works by contemporary Indigenous artists under the title *Unsettled.* Many of the works provided a critical reflection on the exhibition. Included in *Unsettled* was an installation by Indigenous Tasmanian artist Julie Gough titled *Time Keeper* (Figure 6.3). The focal object was a vessel made from kelp filled with sand, not water. It had a hole in the bottom through which the sand trickled, forming a conical pile on the floor. Gough explained that it was 'a statement about time spent apart – between the carrier, its homeland, its people, and its intended purpose'. The artwork was accompanied by a film the artist had made of the beach where the kelp was sourced for the vessel and of her visit to the original water carrier in the British Museum storage facility. She concludes, 'I hope the homeland that the original water carrier hasn't heard for generations can be absorbed by it while in the National Museum of Australia. A bittersweet reunion'.[5]

The Yolngu response to the *baṯi* from Makassar has been very different. It too is likely to be among the oldest objects surviving from that time, at least in museum collections. In the *Encounters* exhibition the Yolngu elder Laklak Burarrwanga produces a historical commentary:

> Long time ago, when the north-east wind blew, the Mangatharra [Makasarese] would travel from their place up north in Indonesia to Arnhem Land. They came in Makassan boats called *praus*. They planted tamarind trees and traded with Aboriginal people. The Aboriginal people, they traded the trepang . . . and the Mangatharra traded knives and material.
>
> (Burarrwanga 2015: 74)

The Yolngu have a sense of continuity with a Macassan past that they do not share with non-Indigenous Australians. Although, as a result of Australian government policy, trade with the Makasarese was stopped over a century ago, relationships with them are maintained through the performance of song cycles, the making of sand sculptures, stone arrangements, ceremonies, and personal names that reference 'Macassan times'. The spear is a sign of a history that Europeans did not know: evidence of trade with Indonesians before European colonization, a record of past journeys and of reconnections that are being made in the present. The same spears are made today for ceremonial performance and traded both within Yolngu society and for sale to outsiders.

The Yolngu work included in the *Unsettled* exhibition did not directly reference the *baṯi*, though such spears are ever present in Yolngu ceremonial performance. The work by Wukun Waṉambi was titled *L̲arrakitj* (Figure 6.4). *L̲arrakitj* is a word for hollow log coffin, the painted hollow

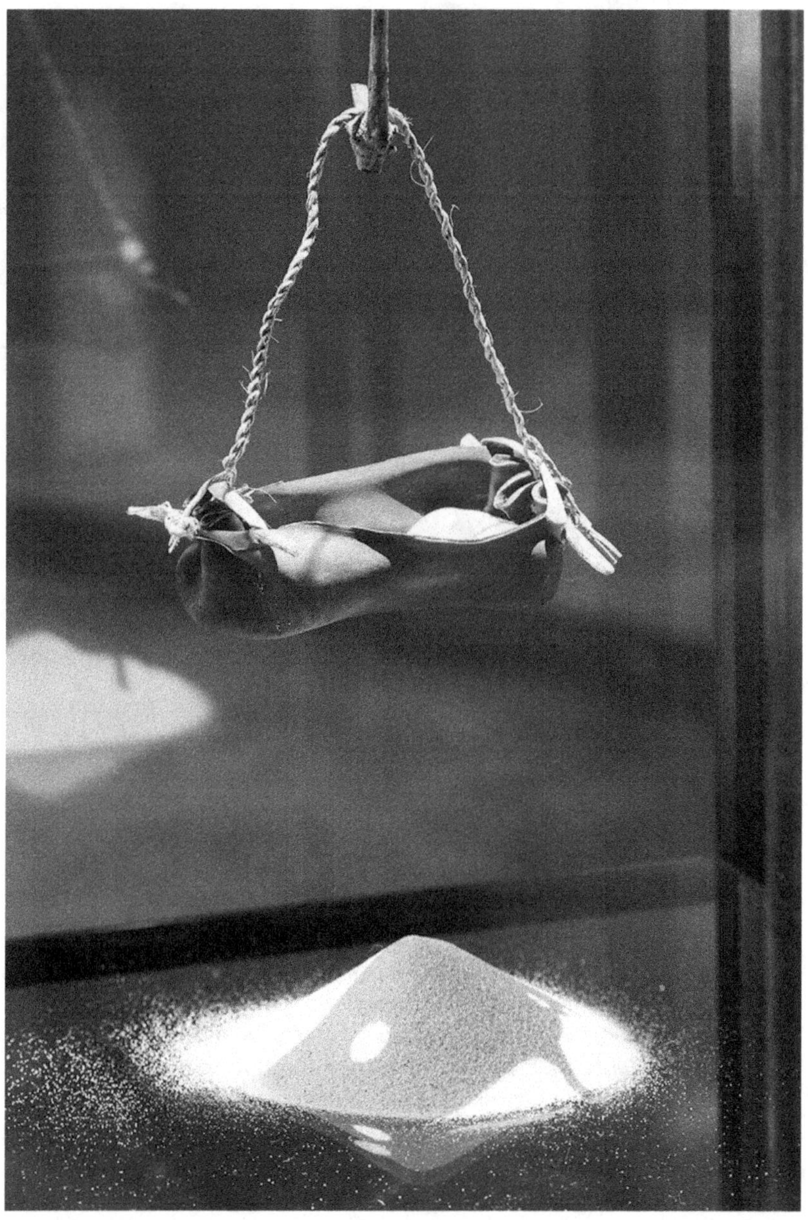

Figure 6.3 *Time Keeper*, 2015, Julie Gough, National Museum of Australia. Bruny Island bull kelp (*Durvillea potatorum*), sand, twigs, and *Lomandra longifolia*, Oyster Cove *Dianella tasmanica*. Photographer, George Serras. Reproduced with permission of the artist and the National Museum of Australia.

Credit: George Serras

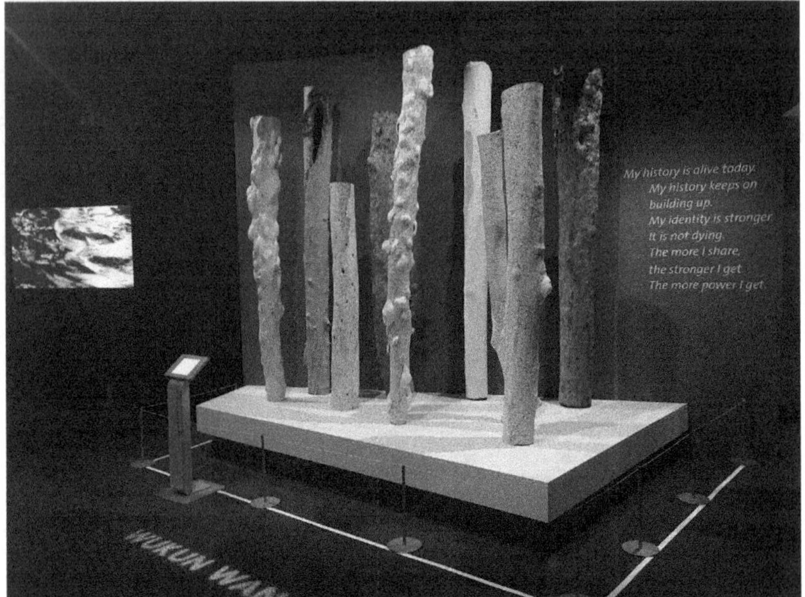

Figure 6.4 Wukun Wa<u>n</u>ambi, *<u>L</u>arrakitj*, 2015. Photographer, Howard Morphy. Reproduced with permission of Buku Larrnggay Mulka, Yirrkala.

Credit: Howard Morphy

stringybark poles that were used as the final resting place for the bones of the dead.

Although bones are no longer dug up for reburial in *<u>l</u>arrakitj*, Yolngu mortuary rituals perform the associated songs and dances in different contexts. *<u>L</u>arrakitj* have become a medium for artistic expression and for communicating Yolngu religious concepts to outsiders. Wukun's installation was almost an exegesis on *<u>l</u>arrakitj*. It comprised a series of hollow trunks, some of which had the straight form traditionally used for the interment of bones and others of irregular shapes. Some of the logs retained their bark, others were stripped clean; some were left unpainted and others were painted with clan designs that would link the deceased person to the spiritual dimension. The objective of the display was to show the process of making *<u>l</u>arrakitj* and the relationship of *<u>l</u>arrakitj* to the forest and the process of growth and decay in the environment. The accompanying text is a reflection on Yolngu metaphysics:

> The outside surface of things hides what is inside. I want to share what is hidden. In Yolngu, understanding the life of the spirit is a circle.

> The *larrakitj* is a circle. We are looking for our identity and we search around and around until we find our destiny and we go straight to that circle and join it and become a part of family.
>
> (Wanambi 2015)[6]

In placing objects in their historical context, it is not my intention to imply that the source communities today, who see the hand and spirit of their ancestors in the collections and archives, belong to different space-times. They are encompassed within the boundaries of the same nation-state – Australia – and subjected to the same policies. The history of the incorporation of different Aboriginal societies within the nation-state has, however, had profoundly different consequences. Indigenous Australians were historically subject to different laws according to state and territory legislation, which has resulted in different frameworks for land rights. Only in rare cases has that resulted in large areas of land being returned to their 'traditional owners' as freehold land. In the better watered regions of southeast Australia, Queensland, and western Australia, most of the land has long been taken out of Aboriginal ownership. For much of the nineteenth and twentieth centuries, Indigenous Australians across the southern part of the continent were invisible to the state, subject to the 'great Australian silence' on their past and presumed to be on a trajectory towards assimilation in the future. While Aboriginal people from central and northern Australia had some prominence as images of what Aboriginal society and way of life had been, there was a strong implication that their way of life belonged to the past, while at the same time providing a challenge to the authenticity and identity of people in the southern states (Fisher 2015).

While historical circumstances for Indigenous Australians differed, from the 1960s onwards, the recognition of rights became a common struggle that united them across the continent in legal and political action. In many respects, the situation has transformed since the 1960s with the passing of a supportive referendum, the implementation in some regions of land rights and native title legislation and a much greater emphasis on the inclusion of Indigenous Australians as part of the political agenda. This recent era has also resulted in a greater recognition and appreciation of Aboriginal performance, visual culture, music, and narrative. Aboriginal art is now integral to the face that Australia presents to the world. Yet at the same time, disadvantage and inequity are strongly felt and many issues remain unresolved.

From a shared present, Indigenous Australians encounter different and relatively autonomous space-times from the past when entering collections and archives and have to connect them with different, though overlapping, trajectories into the present. The collections themselves can seem to be fundamentally different resources in terms of scale, emotional timbre, and potential resource, and priorities in engaging with them are going to vary regionally. But it is important that in the present time, difference is recognized in a collaborative environment in which cultural institutions can work both with that difference and across it.

Reconnections

In recent years, ethnographic collections have become increasingly important as a resource. The present 'museum age' emphasizes collaboration, and the idea that museums are forums for debate and cross-cultural engagement has become widespread. Museum anthropology and ethnographic collections have moved once again into a central position in anthropology. In some respects, museums have become the place where anthropology can be seen to be reconnecting most closely with the Boasian tradition and the cultural relativism of early twentieth-century anthropology. However, this reconnection comes in a new era, where the value creation process is no less important but where globalization, and an emphasis on human rights and technological change has worked together to create an environment in which communities can be central actors.

Indigenous engagement today with collections and archives, in particular in settler-colonial societies, is heightened and intensive and is beginning to utilize all of the skills and resources of the disciplines and institutions that curated, conserved, researched, and displayed the material objects. Yet it is precisely at this moment of engagement that a failure to recognize the value creation process and the multidimensional nature of ethnographic collections can have the effect of deadening discourse by providing simplistic solutions to complex problems.

Perspectives on the past which impose a single interpretative framework create powerful tropes that fix the way an era or phenomenon is understood, making it harder to learn about or learn from the past. The danger is that this masks the process of history and imposes the present on the past. Anthropological and historical arguments lose their subtlety and complexity. The message spreads outside the discipline and can influence the ways in which people in the present engage with institutions that they perceive as being located in the past. In the case of cultural institutions whose greatest resource comes from the past, this can have the effect of devaluing the collections as a future resource. Infinity is constrained and contained. Yet Indigenous engagement with collections in the present has shown how valuable that resource is.

Perhaps the most deadening trope is that of anthropology as the handmaiden of colonialism and the use of ethnographic collections as a main symbol of that connection. That association underlies a series of common assumptions and directions for redress: that museum collections are 'captured heritage'[7]with basements filled with material that was removed without the agency or consent of members of source communities. The implication is that the material – as ill-gotten gains – should be returned from whence it came. Repatriation becomes a dominant focus of critical discourse and media interest. The idea that museum cataloguing systems, by failing to reflect Indigenous ontologies and epistemologies, subordinate the material objects to Western systems of classification linked to evolutionary hierarchies and racial segregation has gained currency. Concerns are raised about the failure of museums to respect Indigenous protocols for access to materials. And from a disciplinary perspective, the idea has gained currency that categorizing and exhibiting material objects as ethnography rather than art is problematic.

Decolonizing the museum

That there is a relationship between anthropology and the history of European colonization is undeniable. As Joshua Bell (2017: 249) puts it, 'Colonialism was and is heterogeneous with a play of agencies defining the periods from which the collections emerged'. Collections provide connections to the people who lived through a history of European colonization. My concern, however, is with the central role given to anthropology in the colonial enterprise. In the current context, the continual placing of anthropology and ethnographic collections in the colonial past is both a misreading of history and a move backwards from the value creation process that has opened up museum collections to a positive engagement with source communities.

It is ironic but not surprising that anthropologists who were, from the perspective of the academy, at the forefront of challenging and opposing race-based ideology subsequently played a leading role in the critique of their own discipline. Talal Asad's 1973 book *Anthropology and the Colonial Encounter* played an important role in establishing the link in the academic imagination. The book itself contained essays that problematized the argument that Asad put forward, but the title tends to be read by people from other disciplines as a factual statement of the involvement of anthropologists in colonial enterprises.

The book was the beginning of a critical turn in anthropology in which a series of books problematized the discipline's past and interrogated its stylistics. The titles were brilliant: Clifford and Marcus *Writing Culture: The Poetics and Politics of Ethnography*, Clifford's *The Predicament of Culture*, and Fabian's *Time and the Other*, and all made valid points, *but* they were welcomed by other disciplines as a refutation of anthropological method and theory.

The subsequent debate within anthropology has been both productive and divisive. Productive because it has made people increasingly conscious of the need to play a more active role in creating a more inclusive world and increase the diversity of participation in the discipline at all levels (Thomas 2018: 394). Productive because most of the research that has been undertaken has failed to sustain the link between anthropology and colonialism in the strong sense, either at the level of theory (Asch 2015; Rodseth 2018; Cowlishaw 2006) or in engagement with colonial administrations (Basu 2016; Fuller 2017; Lewis 2017; Tilley 2011). The divisiveness comes from a tendency to polarize opinions rather than look for common ground. Acknowledging the role that anthropology has played inside and outside the museum in attitudinal change should be perfectly compatible with a recognition that more needs to be done to address the present-day consequences of colonial history (Lowenthal 2009).

Anthropology continued to focus on regional cultures (or to use Nelson Graburn's 1976 term 'fourth world peoples') into a postcolonial era in which nation-states replaced colonial governments across the world. In a sense, anthropology was uncomfortably positioned in that process – precisely because its focus on difference had a different resonance in a post-independence world than it had in the colonial era. The *other* were becoming the citizens of independent nation-states. In settler-colonial societies – in countries such as Australia, Canada, and the USA – where Indigenous people remained in many respects colonized and denied official recognition or autonomy, anthropology had a different resonance, often being associated with a primitive imaginary that positioned Indigenous subjects in the past, thereby challenging their identities in the present.

The critique of anthropology in many ways is a critique of cultural relativism, which can be positioned as situating peoples within colonized societies as *others* and creating boundaries that separate them from the contemporary world of the colonists. Primitivism was opposed to modernity, and modernity was linked to decolonization. Reading anthropology in this light highlights the continuing difficulty that anthropology has in explaining how people are different but arguing that they have to be treated as equals – the same but different. Ethically, there is a difference between a cultural relativism which sees cultures as equal but different and that advocates accommodating difference, from one that sees differences as incommensurable and hierarchically ordered.

So what does decolonizing the museum mean?

Christina Kreps' (2011: 72) summary of what decolonizing the museum involves is

> acknowledging the historical, colonial contingencies under which collections were acquired; revealing Eurocentric ideology and biases in

> the Western museum concept, discourse and practice; [and] acknowledging and including diverse voices and multiple perspectives.

An important thing to note is that this comes from a museum anthropologist and that processes of engagement have a long history in museum anthropology. Indeed, in many ways, the Western museum has been revealed to be a complex and ever-changing 'concept' that emerges in different forms as it articulates over time with global processes and different national agenda (Message 2006; Witcomb 2003). In this book, my focus has been on what I believe perhaps is the one central, unchanging component of the concept – the curation and conservation of collections over time. In the final part of this conclusion, I will reflect on some of those areas of contestation and misinterpretation that divert attention from ways in which museums and collections can be used more beneficially, and to which resources can be more productively directed if the institutions are viewed in the light of their own history and the continuing value of their collections.

Cataloguing and categorizing

In their 2015 article on creating space for Indigenous ontologies, Marisa Elena Duarte and Miranda Belarde-Lewis conclude,

> Specialists must be willing to partner with Native and Indigenous communities and listen to the stories that give meaning to the naming, describing, and organization of documents. Respect for Indigenous holism, political realities, long-term relationship-building, and patience with timelines are essential. Willingness to study Native systems of knowledge in context, to write about them, and to design experimental approaches is integral to shaping the theory that will inform practice.
> (2015: 699)

This could be read as a partial job description for a museum anthropologist – one that already applies. There is fundamental misrecognition of what anthropology does and a fundamental tendency to read colonial and Western epistemologies and ontologies into an approach that is oriented towards the very opposite. The history of anthropology has been one of placing objects and actions in their social and cultural contexts and being cognizant of different worldviews, systems of knowledge and meaning associated with different societies. Indeed, in recent years, one of the key areas of debate has been over different ontologies and their commensurability (see e.g. Boelstrof 2016). Indeed, as Duarte and Belarde-Lewis (2015: 678) write, 'Understanding distinctiveness leads us to appreciate how "we are all the same, differently."'[8]

Cataloguing and documentation systems are much misunderstood, and the very methods and approaches of museum anthropologists are often the ones that members of source communities want to have in place. There is often a desire for fuller documentation, easier access, and sometimes a revision of terminology, but those desires can be taken on board as part of the core business of the institutions. In a recent essay, Gwyneira Isaacs (2015: 298–299) quotes Jim Enote, the head of the A:shiwi A:wan Museum, on the ideal museum practice being

> when a group of people document the object adding different perspectives and enriching the digital catalogue, providing information on the name or names of the object, its material composition, the groups to which it belongs, who made it and so on.

He states, 'We want to be part of shaping and contributing to the field of museology and information science – however that turns out'.

A key issue that museums and researchers share with source communities, and indeed with users of museums and archives in general, is the history of the dispersal and disaggregation of material objects (Chapter 7). Bringing collections together is an essential step in most research projects but is often also an important project for many source communities, creating a virtual collection from material that has been curated in different institutions.

It is important to distinguish between the cataloguing, categorizing, and documenting of collections. The primary objective of cataloguing is to help people to find and locate objects in collections. The categories that are developed in the process of cataloguing make items discoverable through a process of systematic and generic labelling. A catalogue should reflect the interests of people who are using the collection, help them to find objects of interest to them, and help them to relate those objects to others in the collection. Catalogues are likely to be used for many different purposes, from enabling people to find material and research the collection, to auditing the institution and valuing the collection. Key categories are likely to include the time and place of the collection, maker, culture, and object type. And in the present era, categorical metadata should allow people to search across different institutions, both nationally and globally.

In cataloguing ethnographic collections, it is clearly important that Indigenous terminologies and relevant data be included in the documentation. Museum cataloguing systems should facilitate research with reference to key cultural categories and concepts of source communities. It is important that Indigenous societies are classified by the name by which they recognize themselves and that key organizational features of each society are included in drop-down menus. This is because, from the point of view of the Indigenous user, categories vary regionally. Categories salient to a particular community of origin need to be explored with that community and then generally agreed across institutions. Then the material objects from that community should be documented according to the desired categories and culturally intuitive search terms. For example, within Australia, some Indigenous societies are organized on the basis of moieties and others are not. The catalogues of institutions with significant Australian collections need to build those categories into their systems and apply them appropriately. Devising appropriate terminology will always be a work in progress that responds to the different interests and requirements of users of collections.

It is necessary to distinguish between the task of documenting objects held in particular institutions and the issue of finding objects and collections that are associated with particular source communities which are dispersed through many institutions. The latter process needs to be iterative, involving the source communities, museum curators in many institutions, and researchers. Before material can be documented in ways that are relevant to the source communities, it has to be found. The museum's task is to create a cataloguing system, based on existing and often limited information about the objects they hold, that allows those objects to come up in a search. The Yolngu, who look for objects in collections by searching on the basis of moiety, are unlikely to find many, because the moiety names are seldom part of existing documentation. They are much more likely to find material on the basis of more general terms referring to locations within Australia, such as the Northern Territory or Arnhem Land, or 'Australian Aboriginal'. Once an object is found by the source community, it becomes possible to set up relationships between them and the museums that hold their objects. In turn, these relationships will ensure that, over time, the perspective of source communities are reflected in the documentation of their objects in museum collections, and museum catalogues are refined to make them more easily searchable by interested members of source communities.

The categories employed in cataloguing do reflect the era in which a catalogue was made. The categories used in mediaeval, Enlightenment and contemporary times are going to differ markedly, as they will differ on the basis of nationality, disciplinary focus, and sectional interest. Catalogues invariably suffer from time lag; they take a long time to develop, and replacing them is a major task. The danger is that labels stick, and people using them need to be aware of the danger of old terminologies that have connotations that belong to past categorization of people on the basis of race, nationality, religious affiliation, occupation, and so on. Many labels need to be changed. But the previous categorizations need to be preserved as documentation. They are sources of information about history, reflect orderings in times past, and are part of the accumulated layering of history that builds the archive and adds to the value of the objects. Categories and priorities change, but the object as an identity, as something that can be found and continually revisited, remains.

Recognition, access, engagement, and repatriation

The order of this heading is significant. The need is to build people's agency over the collection into the present and that is very much a process that is underway. In practice, physical repatriation is the desired solution for only some communities and only a small proportion of objects within ethnographic collections, but the rhetoric surrounding repatriation has often implied that museums are withholding objects from communities – who all want them back. The difficulty with this rhetoric is that it masks and even undermines the collaborative relationships that have been developing between museums and source communities over several decades. And it fails to address what happens when objects are returned to source communities – how are the collections going to be resourced, conserved, accessed, and used as a community resource without substantial funding.

In recent decades, access to collections has been transformed though digital technology. Digital catalogues and databases have made it much easier for people to undertake the initial stage of locating items held in distributed collections. Online communication creates the possibility of contacting curators and collection managers in distant places. Digital technology has also opened up the possibility of what is generally referred to as 'digital repatriation' in the form of high-quality images and recordings, including 3D images and digital printing. These changes have transformed what is possible and what is desired. Finding where collections are and bringing them together virtually enables access, and it also enables the resource to be distributed widely within the community. Digital repatriation has the advantage of enabling the object, whether it is a sound recording, fragile document, or material culture object to continue to be curated within the museum's collections for future access and research.

There clearly is a difference between the actual object and what is essentially a reproduction or copy. Whether dealing with sound recordings, photographs, letters, notebooks, or artefacts, the original object has more potential value than the copies generated from it. The material object has much greater research potential. From an exhibition perspective, the original object has a presence that cannot be replicated through reproductions. And, clearly, from the perspective of the source community, it has a much deeper and more direct connection to the hand that made it and to the context of use than a digital image. However, experience has shown in recent years that communities are more focussed on having direct access to images than to material objects, except in particular cases. Digital images can be archived, accessed by many people, reproduced in different formats, and modified and repurposed. Source communities are as sensitive to the aspiration of long-term conservation as members of the museum community. And, increasingly, source communities are interested in the developing research potential of material objects whether through enhancing the sound of early recordings, reconstructing damaged objects, or identifying the hand of the maker or the group ownership of an item.

The issue of repatriation has become heated in recent years and is often put in the same frame as decolonization, almost as if it were a solution to present inequities and past histories of colonial violence and appropriation. In recent years, some governments have seen it as an instrument in global diplomacy and, in the case of Indigenous populations within settler-colonial societies, as a means of returning agency to Indigenous communities. However, there is no evidence that the return of objects from ethnographic collections to the communities of origin is, in most cases, a great priority.

My concern is that far from being a solution to a problem or remedying an injustice, repatriation as a general policy initiative is going to have the opposite effect to that intended. I have three main worries: one is the threat to museum collections as a whole; the second is a pragmatic concern that people have failed to take account of the scale of the collections and the costs of repatriation; the third is that a general policy of repatriation fails to take account of the particular histories of source communities and the spatio-temporal disjunctions that exist. Entangled in all three factors is an implicit theory or hope that the return of cultural materials can in a sense reverse process of history. There is a danger of giving agency back to descendants as if they were living in an imagined past rather than in the present. None of this excludes the possibility, however, that in particular cases, repatriation will be the best and ethically most appropriate outcome.

My concern about museum collections is, in a sense, the topic of every chapter. My initial premise is that museum collections are valuable resources that have been created over centuries, and like many other scarce resources, they should be maintained for the future. That does not mean that all objects have to remain in the museum but that the vast majority are likely to. The collections have multiple values invested in them, and in the case of ethnographic collections, they played a major role in attitudinal change. That role is an ongoing one that has to continue to operate on a global and national basis. The national and global presence of ethnographic material culture as a valued expression of the diversity of human creativity is not only an assertion of value but also can provide a platform for source communities to gain visibility and recognition and assert their rights to autonomy.

An unintended consequence of the rhetoric of repatriation is that it may inhibit adding to collections in the future or at least redirect resources towards particular safe niches. The vast majority of objects in the museum entered through trade and exchange or as gifts. That trade is ongoing, and the gifts are a way of bringing private collections into the public domain. The investment of resources in national museums and archives has been one of the main reasons why material objects from the past have survived into the present to be reconnected to source communities. In Australia, the recent strong Indigenous engagement with museum collections and the recognition of the aesthetic and cultural significance of Indigenous art has resulted in a further growth of collections and their spread into art museums.

The scale of material in collections is enormous. The curation of collections is an expensive project, and it is unlikely that most source communities will have the resources to curate and conserve the collections or that the conservation of repatriated collections will be a priority. Few local communities have the resources to invest in local museums or keeping houses and the resources provided by governments tend to be minimal. Often, the rarest objects, such as the Tasmanian kelp water carrier, are the ones that are closest to grasping at infinity, conserving an infinite possibility of knowledge and bringing people close to a distant past. And the rarest objects require the greatest resources to conserve them and deserve the most attention. Return often means the shift of responsibility away from government and public institutions to local communities and the history of long-term support is not good.

The rhetoric of repatriation tends to focus on objects leaving the museum and far less on where they are going and how they are going to be reconnected to cultures of origin. Repatriation is as much about connections to people as it is to place. Indeed, in many cases, the distributed nature of communities matches the distributed nature of collections. Connections need to be made in the context of people's present lives. Source communities at a national and even regional level cannot be conceived of as fixed and bounded entities but as sets of people with different histories. Many communities comprise internal diaspora across the nation and include people who speak different languages, hold different religious beliefs, and imagine different futures.

Imagining alternatives to repatriation

The presence of Indigenous cultures and histories in state and national institutions is vital for both Indigenous and non-Indigenous people alike. And on an international basis given the ongoing migrations that have occurred during the colonial era, it is clearly important for the African, Asian, American, and Pacific diaspora in Europe and America to have direct links to their countries of origin. Many Indigenous Australians have strong links to the United Kingdom and the presence of Indigenous collections in European are clearly seen to be an important asset.

There are always going to be hard cases and ones in which very different and even conflicting values need to be taken into account. In cases where the destruction of the object is the intended outcome, it is important that sufficient time is taken by everyone involved to reflect on the consequences for future generations and whether there are ways to accommodate both present interests and possible futures. My hope is that museums and their source communities work to ensure physical repatriation to source communities does not become the singular solution to the entwined histories of museums and colonialism. Over time, processes involving long-term loans, co-curation, co-ownership, and, in some cases, transfer of ownership can be put in place. Such arrangements will need to be built into a dynamic and well-resourced institutional structure that will allow the collections to be conserved and remain available for future uses. Networked connections between national museums, regional museums, and local cultural or keeping centres will be part of this structure. Today, source communities, in many cases, share Yolngu views of the wisdom of previous generations who saw museums as a means to conserve their heritage, not with a short-term view in mind but as a means for objects to have a continuing life inside and, in different forms, outside the museum.

Noongar ethnomusicologist Clint Bracknell has, in his own words, been 'hunting the songs' from his country in Southern Western Australia. The region was colonized early on in the European settlement of Western Australia. Today, there are 40,000 people of Noongar descent but fewer than 100 speakers of the language, though language revival is well underway. The song traditions that, he argues, were an integral part of language that ceased to be passed on. Images and accounts from the past show the richness of the ceremonial performance, but the sound is largely missing. However, in working through collections in different archives recordings are being uncovered, and he has led a project working with researchers and community members to bring the music back. The connection with the past is palpable in what is preserved in the archives:

> In their act of performing the songs, the 'informants' signaled the importance of their preservation and transmission to future generations, perhaps because of the significant role that this music could play in the maintenance of individual and collective Noongar identity.
>
> (Bracknell 2014: 11)

Bracknell concludes by reflecting on the dialogical relationship that exists between the search for knowledge and the maintenance of a particular 'Indigenous standpoint':

> Adopting such a methodological process may in turn lead researchers to articulate and apply unique, 'hitherto submerged' epistemological perspectives, to extend discourses and disciplines, adapt old methodologies, or invent totally new approaches to specifically serve Indigenous interests.
>
> (Ibid)

Yolngu researchers working through museum collections have a vast distributed archive to work with and have in recent years been strongly engaged with institutions. This has enabled them to add to documentation and emphasize the key categories that are important to them – including, for example, the names of the relevant clan and moiety affiliation (Gumbula et al. 2009; Hamby and Gumbula 2015). The collections in turn have provided vital information about the recent past that has been incorporated in current practice, ceremonial performance, and legal cases (see Chapter 3). The Yolngu have also been centrally involved in curating exhibitions, from a Yolngu perspective, which have brought together objects from many different institutions (Morphy 2010).[9]

Last words

Museums contain infinite resources in the form of their collections, but they can also be dynamic institutions and instruments of change. The reciprocal of bringing material home to source communities has been a reaching out by Indigenous communities to cultural institutions within their nation-states and across international boundaries. In a time of rapid change, the diaspora of museum objects provides an extraordinary resource for global connection of people with their collections and between different Indigenous communities. It is going to take time to develop the structures that enable access, and because of the complexity of the issues involved, they are developing organically.

Source communities, researchers, and curators working with archives and collections have many shared objectives, and this has opened avenues for collaborative and mutually beneficial relationships. It is important, in collaborative projects, that the knowledge of members of source communities is recognized as equivalent to the knowledge others bring, and that this is reflected in the funding. Most projects that are being developed now emphasize collaboration and provide a mechanism for recognizing the contribution that Indigenous knowledge systems can make in the contemporary world. Arguably, museums and archives are among the main domains in which Indigenous cultures are playing a central role in the contemporary world.

Partnerships and sharing of resources and knowledge are part of the process. But it is important to create the space and time for remade connections to be established in place. In some cases, the space-time disjunctions are not as profound. In others, time needs to be allowed for the source communities to manage the new opportunities presented. The struggle for recognition, access, reconnection, and, in some cases, return requires considerable investments in time, but once reconnection has been achieved, space and time have to be created within the community and in individual lives for relationships to be remade. The space needed for reengagement will differ radically according to the nature of the spatio-temporal gap between collections and the present, the nature of the colonial encounter, and the emotional timbre and sometimes contested nature of the material concerned.

As Palawa artist and curator Julie Gough writes: 'My return to Tasmania, was and is not a moment but is ongoing – something I think is important to consider also regarding returned ancestors' remains and cultural objects – this being that disrupted time/place/relationships cannot be fixed or set- right overnight' (http://fashiondocbox.com/66048777-Body_Art/Dr-julie-gough-wac8-thursday-1-sept-pm-room-r302-doshisha-university-kyoto.html).

Notes

1 Indeed, Michael Asch (2015) has argued that the transformation in conception of human time during the course of the nineteenth century from a biblical framework of God's creation to a geological and evolutionary framework was a significant factor in the value creation process that a comparative anthropology engaged in. While Morgan's evolutionism distanced diverse cultures in the present, he argues that the different relativisms of Boasian particularism and Radcliffe-Brownian structural functionalism 'proved of great value in helping to move the world community to the understanding that, counter to the position justifying colonialism, all ways of life and all peoples are equal in standing. Indeed, it remains of value today as a counter to those who denigrate Indigenous (and other) ways of life by describing them as somehow inferior to our own' (Asch 2015: 486).

2 The changeover of exhibitions was slower than originally intended, and it lasted from 1972–1982.

3 Mountford suggested that the spear might have come from Groote Eylandt. However, the black painted barb is characteristic of spears from the neighbouring Yolngu people of Blue Mud Bay, and it is as likely that it comes from that region as from Groote Eylandt.

4 For detailed reflections on these two exhibitions, see Morphy (2015, 2017).

5 The artist's statement is taken form the National Museum's web entry on the exhibition, consulted on 25 December 2018, www.nma.gov.au/exhibitions/unsettled/julie_gough.

6 www.nma.gov.au/exhibitions/unsettled/wukun-wanambi.

7 The title of Cole's (1985) book, *Captured Heritage: The Scramble for Northwest Coast Artifacts*, Vancouver University of British Columbia Press – a book that in many ways presents a nuanced picture of the development of museum collections that the title fixes in a particular direction and that fails to see the value-creation processes that the museums were engaged in (a fact acknowledged in effect by his preface to the second edition published in 1985, which shows the process of engagement with communities that was underway).

8 Here they are quoting Manulani Aluli Meyer's "Indigenous Knowledge: Stories of Relationship and Resurgence." Presentation at the Intersectionality Research, Policy and Practice Conference, Vancouver, British Columbia, 2014.

9 One of the most innovative exhibitions was Dr Joe Gumbula's 2010 *Makarr-garma: Aboriginal Collections from a Yolngu Perspective* at the University of Sydney's Macleay Museum.

References

Asad, T. (ed) (1973) *Anthropology & the Colonial Encounter*, New York: Humanities Press.

Asch, M. (2015) "Anthropology, colonialism and the reflexive turn: finding a place to stand," *Anthropologica*, 57 (2): 481–489.

Atto, T. (2015) *In National Museum of Australia Encounters*, Canberra: National Museum of Australia.

Basu, P. (2016) "N.W. Thomas and colonial anthropology in British West Africa: reappraising a cautionary tale," *Journal of the Royal Anthropological Institute*, (N.S.) 22: 84–107.

Bell, J. (2017) "A bundle of relations: collections, collecting, communities," *Annual Review of Anthropology*, 46: 241–259.

Boelstrof, T. (2016) "For whom the ontology turns," *Current Anthropology*, 57 (4): 387–407.

Bracknell, C. (2014) "Wal-Walang-al Ngardanginy: hunting the songs," *Australian Aboriginal Studies*, 1: 3–15.

Burarrwanga, L. (2015) *In National Museum of Australia Encounters*, Canberra: National Museum of Australia.

Cole, D. (1985) *Captured Heritage*, Vancouver: UBC Press.

Cowlishaw, G. (2006) "On 'getting it wrong': collateral damage in the history wars," *Australian Historical Studies*, 37 (127): 181–202.

Duarte, M. and Belarde-Lewis, M. (2015) "Imagining: creating spaces for indigenous ontologies," *Cataloging & Classification Quarterly*, 53 (5–6): 677–702.

Fisher, L. (2015) *Aboriginal Art and Society: Hope and Disenchantment*, London: Anthem Press.

Fuller, C.J. (2017) "Ethnographic inquiry in colonial India: Herbert Risley, William Crooke, and the study of tribes and castes," *Journal of the Royal Anthropological Institute*, (N.S.) 23: 603–621.

Graburn, N. (1976) Ethnic and Tourist Arts: Cultural Expressions from the Fourth World, Berkeley: University of California Press.

Gumbula, N., Corn, A. and Mant, J. (2009) "Matjabala Mali' Buku-Runganmaram: implications for archives and access in Arnhem Land," *Journal of Archival Science*, 9: 7–14.

Hamby, L. and Gumbula, J. (2015) "Development of collecting at Milingimbi mission," in Toner, P. (ed) *Strings of Connectedness: Essays in Honour of Ian Keen*, pp. 187–214, Canberra: ANU Press.

Isaac, G. (2015) " 'Get to know your world': an interview with Jim Enote, Director of the A:shiwi A:wan Museum and Heritage Center," in Coombes, A. and Philip, R.B. (eds) *Museum Transformations*, pp. 289–311, London: Routledge.

Kreps, C. (2011) "Changing the rules of the road: postcolonialism and the new ethics of museum anthropology," in Marstine, J. (ed) *The Routledge Companion to Museum Ethics: Redefining Ethics for the Twenty-First-Century Museum*, pp. 70–85, London: Routledge.

Lewis, H.S. (2017) *In Defense of Anthropology: An Investigation of the Critique of Anthropology*, Abingdon: Routledge.

Lowenthal, D. (2009) "On arraigning ancestors: a critique of historical contrition," *North Carolina Law Review*, 87 (3): 901–966.

Message, K. (2006) *New Museums and the Making of Culture*, Oxford: Berg.

Morphy, H. (2007) *Becoming Art: Exploring Cross-Cultural Categories*, Oxford: Berg.

Morphy, H. (2010) " 'Not just pretty pictures': relative autonomy and the articulations of Yolngu art in its contexts," in Strang, V. and Busse, M. (eds) *Ownership and Appropriation*, pp. 261–286, Oxford: Berg.

Morphy, H. (2015) "Indigenous Australia: enduring civilisation, a personal reflection," *Museum Worlds: Advances in Research*, 3 (1): 7–17.

Morphy, H. (2017) "Encounters at the National Museum of Australia: a moment in an ongoing process of engagement," *International Journal of Heritage Studies*, 23 (9): 875–878.

Oscar, J. (2015) "Encountering truth: the real life stories of objects from empire's frontier and beyond," *National Museum of Australia Encounters*, 22–27.

Rodseth, L. (2018) "Hegemonic concepts of culture: the checkered history of dark anthropology," *The American Anthropologist*, 120 (3): 398–411.

Thomas, D.A. (2018) "Decolonising disciplines," *American Anthropologist*, 120 (3): 393–397.

Tilley, H. (2011) *Africa as a Living Laboratory: Empire, Development, and the Problem of Scientific Knowledge, 1870–1950*, Chicago: University of Chicago Press.

Wanambi, W. 2015 Wukun Wanambi Unsettled: stories within National Museum of Australia https://www.nma.gov.au/exhibitions/unsettled/wukun-wanambi consulted 18 September 2019

Witcomb, A. (2003) *Re-Imagining the Museum: Beyond the Mausoleum*, London: Routledge.

Index